Plain English Series:

Spelling

by Kathleen Knoblock

illustrated by
Renée Yates

FS-10171 Plain English Series: Spelling
All rights reserved–Printed in the U.S.A.
Copyright © 1995 Frank Schaffer Publications, Inc.
23740 Hawthorne Blvd.
Torrance, CA 90505

Plain English is a no-nonsense series designed to be used with students aged nine through adult who need instruction or reinforcement in basic English communication. *Spelling* contains a selection of 11 skills common in everyday speaking and writing, but often confused or misused.

Table of Contents

Flow Chart

A flow chart is a useful tool for organizing your teaching and helping ensure that students reach skill mastery. The chart below outlines an effective approach for teaching the skills in this book using the materials provided.

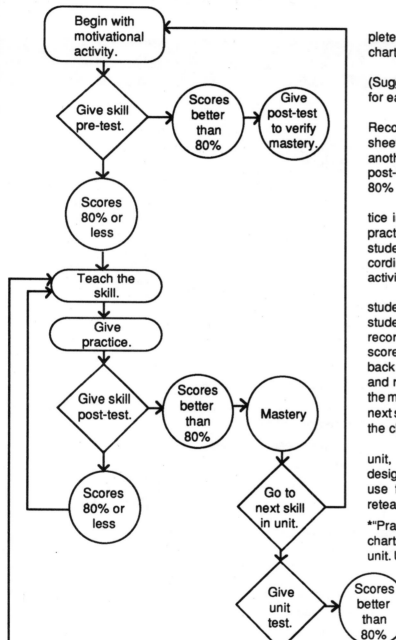

Plain English—Spelling contains a complete 11-skill unit. Follow the steps in this flow chart to teach the skills in the unit.

Begin a lesson with a motivational activity. (Suggestions are given on the teaching pages for each skill.)

After introducing the skill, give the pre-test. Record the results on students' individual record sheets. If a student scores better than 80% (or another mastery level that you choose), give the post-test to verify mastery. If a student scores 80% or less, proceed to teach the skill.*

After direct instruction, give students practice in applying the skill. This book contains a practice sheet for each skill which can be done by students working together or individually. Recording the scores on the record sheet for this activity is optional.

Following instruction and practice, give students the post-test. Record the results on students' individual record sheets. Using the record sheets, form a group of students who scored 80% or less on the post-test; then go back and reteach the skill. Give more practice and repeat the post-test. When students reach the mastery level on the post-test, proceed to the next skill in the unit, beginning again at the top of the chart.

After teaching each of the 11 skills in the unit, give students the unit test. This test is designed to assess mastery in context. Again, use the test results to group students; then reteach any skills not yet mastered.

*"Practice With a Purpose," a section of mini-charts that correspond with the skills, follows the unit. Use these versatile pages to teach, reteach, and provide additional practice and follow-up for each skill. Make transparencies from them, use them as file folder centers, or reproduce them to make individual student rule/practice books, or copy the exercises onto chart paper for group work.

Teachers often face the frustrating problem of having some students who have mastered a skill before it is taught, others who learn it from direct instruction, and still others who require reteaching and review. Here are some classroom-tested ideas for dealing with this problem. These ideas will help ensure that all students get the instruction they need, simplify your record keeping, and increase your accountability.

Terrific Teaching Tips

Teaching "By the Numbers"

Have each student keep an individual record sheet (page 95).

Tip! Assign each student a student number. An easy way to do this is to go in order down your class list. Have students put their numbers as well as their names on all work.

Tip! Each time an assessment is made, sort the students by number to group for teaching. For example, assume you have 30 students numbered 1–30. You have given the pre-test for a skill. (If your students can record their scores themselves, have them do it!) You know you will have to teach the skill to some, but probably not all, of your students. Quickly sort through the assessment papers, removing all those with scores better than 80% (or another mastery level that you have chosen). You now have two sets of papers. In your plan book jot down the numbers of the students who need direct instruction.

Tip! Copy only the number of practice pages needed. (This will save time and resources by eliminating the duplicating of unnecessary pages.) When you are ready to teach the skill, call out the numbers of the students who are to join the instructional group.

Cozy Clusters

After the directed lesson and practice, give the post-test to all students. Repeat the sorting process when planning a reteaching lesson. Again, prepare materials only for students who need them. Record keeping is simplified further because in your previous sorting you already separated the record sheets of those students.

Another way to group for instruction is to give several or all of the pre-tests before beginning any formal instruction. Then, sort the completed record sheets by skill mastery and teach skills in clusters. Perhaps you have students who have mastered most or all of the skills. Check by giving these students the unit test.

Skill Growth Portfolio

Help students take pride in their achievements and instill in them a greater sense of responsibility by having them create a skill growth portfolio in which they keep their tests, practice papers, and record sheets. This not only relieves you of that duty, but allows students to track their own progress and be more actively involved in their own learning.

Tip! Have students make their own rule books to keep in their portfolios as they work through the skills. (See idea below.) Have students copy the rules as you teach them or use the "Practice With a Purpose" mini-charts in one of the ways described below.

"Practice With a Purpose" Mini-charts

"Practice With a Purpose" is a special section of mini-charts designed to provide extra opportunities to extend and reinforce skills. It includes a ready-to-use rule page for lessons and reference, plus a practice page for application and follow-up for each skill. First, a "rule of thumb" is given in simple language along with correct (✓) and incorrect (✗) examples. Then, the practice page provides an additional opportunity to apply the skill in context. Here are a few ways to use these special pages.

• Overhead Transparencies and Charts

Copy the rules and/or practice activity onto chart paper for small group instruction. After the lesson, post the chart as a reference for students.

Make a set of rule and practice transparencies directly from the pages. Use the rule transparency to teach or reteach the skill. Then use the practice transparency to have students record on paper their responses to the exercises presented on the overhead screen. Correct the activity together. After marking the answers in grease pencil, simply wipe the transparency clean and it is ready to use again.

• Rule and Practice File Folder Centers

Make a photocopy of each skill's rule and practice pages. Mount the copies side-by-side in a file folder. Write the skill on the tab. These folders can be posted or placed in a box for students to complete independently.

• Individual Student Rule and Practice Books

Have students copy rules from charts, transparencies, or file folders to make their own rule books. The following page provides a reproducible rule book template (with space for students to write the rule and practice answers). Or, reproduce the rule and practice pages directly for students to compile into books.

Spelling—By the Rules

Name _____ **Date** _____

Skill _____

_____

_____

_____

_____

_____

_____

_____

Rule of Thumb

Examples (✗ incorrect; ✓ correct)

✗ _____

✓ _____

✗ _____

✓ _____

Practice

1. _____

2. _____

3. _____

4. _____

5. _____

Related materials for teaching Spelling: *Its* and *It's*
Reproducible: Pre-test and Post-test (page 12); Practice Page (page 11)
Enrichment Activity (page 10)
Rule Book Template (page 6); Individual Record Sheet (page 95)
"Practice With a Purpose": Sound-Alikes *Its* and *It's* (pages 73-74)

Spelling: *Its* and *It's*

The ideas on these three pages follow the flow chart of suggested steps for teaching, reteaching, and testing presented on page 3 of this book.

STEP 1:
Motivation—What Is Its Meaning?

Introduce the skill by writing several sentences containing the words *its* and *it's* used correctly. Ask students to tell what the word means in each sentence. Here are some suggested sentences:

- I think **It's** going to rain. *(it is)*
- The pot is missing **Its** handle. *(belongs to it)*
- **It's** the brightest star. *(it is)*
- This shirt lost **Its** color. *(belongs to it)*
- **It's** too hot to sleep. *(it is)*
- **Its** cage is big enough. *(belongs to it)*
- **It's** been a long time. *(it has)*

Its cage is empty!

It's escaping!

STEP 2:
Pre-test and Grouping for Instruction

It is likely that at some time in their writing, your students have misspelled *its* or *it's*. Follow the brief oral introduction above by giving all students the written pre-test (page 12). Record (or have students record) their scores on an individual record sheet (page 95). Sort through the record sheets and remove the tests of students who scored 100%. You may choose to give these students the post-test right away to verify mastery or wait to give it to them with the rest of the class. Form a group of students who scored 80% or lower for direct instruction and practice.

STEP 3:
Instruction

Students who need instruction in this skill are not yet able to differentiate between *its* and *it's* in written context. These students are probably unaware of the difference in speaking as well. Because the two words sound the same in speech, these students do not perceive the misuse in writing. (See chart below. This visual comparison may help students see the difference they are unable to hear.)

BELONGS TO	IS / HAS
his her Its	he's she's It's

Draw a blank two-column table like the one shown. Introduce the skill by writing the following words in the first column and asking students what they mean: *his, hers, its.* (belongs to him, belongs to her, belongs to it). Write *BELONGS TO* at the head of the column. Next, write *he's, she's,* and *it's* in the second column. Again, ask students what each one means (she is or she has, he is or he has, it is or it has). Write *IS / HAS* at the top of the second column.

Present students with the same sentences used in the motivational activity or other examples using *its* and *it's*. Ask them if the word *its / it's* in the sentence means *belongs to it* or *it is / has*. Have students create a general rule for recognizing and differentiating between *its* and *it's*. (If you are using "Practice With a Purpose" coordinated mini-charts, use the rule page for this lesson.)

You may want students to copy and keep the rhyming rule given below. Help students discern the correct spelling of this troublesome pair by telling them to use the rule to test each sentence they write that contains *its* or *it's*.

RULE 1
☞

Its and **It's** may give you fits,
But just remember this:
If it "belongs to it" use *ITS*.
If "it is" or "it has" use *IT'S*.

STEP 4:
Apply and Practice

Following direct instruction, give students the opportunity to apply the skill in practice. You may use the prepared practice sheet provided (page 11), side two of the "Practice With a Purpose" mini-chart (page 74), or your own practice sentences. Students can use plain writing paper to copy and correct sentences you write on the board or those provided on the mini-chart. If you choose to use the reproducible practice sheet, duplicate only the number needed for your instructional group. (Use the pre-test results to determine the exact number of students who will need practice.)

Practice may be guided or done independently. Students may work individually, in pairs, or as a group. Correct the page together or privately to assess the need for reteaching before giving the post-test.

STEP 5:
Post-test and Reteaching

When your students have had sufficient instruction and practice, give the post-test. After recording scores on the individual record sheets, once again separate the sheets of those students who scored 80% or less on the post-test for reteaching. You may use or reuse any of the materials suggested in Step 4 for reteaching.

Follow-up / Enrichment

Once students have mastered the skill, make certain they retain it by giving a follow-up activity several weeks later. An excellent way to do this is to see if they can identify errors and apply the skill in context. At the right is a story you can copy onto chart paper to check for retention. Or, if you prefer, use the prepared reproducible activity sheet on the following page. Have students fill in the blanks with *its* or *it's*. **Tip!** Students may enjoy writing a description of a food they particularly like or dislike.

To be corrected

It's Not That I Don't Like Them

_____ not that I don't like them. _____ not so much the taste; _____ the way one feels in my mouth. My tongue doesn't like _____ squishy texture or the way _____ shaped. There's also that powdery coating. After I eat one, _____ all over my lips!

"_____ better when _____ roasted!" a friend told me. So I gave it another chance. I stuck _____ mushy body on a stick and roasted it over a fire. Well, let me tell you this. _____ soft white surface turned lumpy and burnt. _____ insides tasted like glue and it attached itself to my teeth.

I guess _____ time to admit the truth. I just don't like marshmallows.

Corrected

It's Not That I Don't Like Them

It's not that I don't like them. **It's** not so much the taste; **it's** the way one feels in my mouth. My tongue doesn't like **its** squishy texture or the way **it's** shaped. There's also that powdery coating. After I eat one, **it's** all over my lips!

"**It's** better when **it's** roasted!" a friend told me. So I gave it another chance. I stuck **its** mushy body on a stick and roasted it over a fire. Well, let me tell you this. **Its** soft white surface turned lumpy and burnt. **Its** insides tasted like glue and it attached itself to my teeth.

I guess **it's** time to admit the truth. I just don't like marshmallows.

ANSWER KEYS

Pre-test:	Practice:		Post-test:
1. B) It's	1. A) its	6. B) it's	1. B) It's
2. A) its	2. A) Its	7. B) It's	2. A) Its
3. A) its	3. A) its	8. B) It's	3. A) Its
4. B) it's	4. B) It's	9. A) its	4. B) It's
5. B) it's	5. A) Its	10. A) Its	5. B) It's

**Practice With a Purpose—
Sound-Alikes *It's* and *Its***

1. It's great . . .
2. correct
3. correct
4. Its wings . . .
5. It's cold . . .

Spelling *Its* and *It's*

Read the story. Use the rules you have learned about *its* and *it's* to decide which spelling belongs in each blank. Then copy the story completed correctly on the lines below.

It's Not That I Don't Like Them

____ not that I don't like them. ____ not so much the taste; ____ the way one feels in my mouth. My tongue doesn't like ____ squishy texture or the way ____ shaped. There's also that powdery coating. After I eat one, ____ all over my lips!

"____ better when ____ roasted!" a friend told me. So I gave it another chance. I stuck ____ mushy body on a stick and roasted it over a fire. Well, let me tell you this. ____ soft white surface turned lumpy and burnt. ____ insides tasted like glue and it attached itself to my teeth.

I guess ____ time to admit the truth. I just don't like marshmallows.

_____

_____

_____

_____

_____

_____

_____

_____

_____

_____

_____

_____

_____

_____

Sound-Alikes *Its* and *It's*

Directions: Think about the meaning of each sentence. Decide if *its* or *it's* belongs in the blank. Write *A* or *B* on the line.

What Is It?

_____ 1. It never speaks but you answer _____ call. A) its B) it's

_____ 2. _____ teeth grip but never bite. A) Its B) It's

_____ 3. It has no head but you can read _____ face. A) its B) it's

_____ 4. _____ invisible but always there. A) Its B) It's

_____ 5. _____ eye never sees. A) Its B) It's

_____ 6. You never wear it but _____ often put on
or taken off. A) its B) it's

_____ 7. _____ dark but only seen in the light. A) Its B) It's

_____ 8. _____ "thrown" but never caught. A) Its B) It's

_____ 9. You eat _____ ears. A) its B) it's

_____ 10. _____ head and foot are never on the floor. A) Its B) It's

Riddle answers:

1) telephone 2) zipper 3) clock 4) air 5) needle 6) weight 7) a shadow 8) a party 9) corn 10) bed

Sound-Alikes *Its* and *It's*

Directions: Think about the meaning of each sentence. Decide if *its* or *it's* belongs in the blank. Write *A* or *B* on the line.

_____ 1. _____ common to have a dog for a pet.
    A) Its   B) It's

_____ 2. A dog is often affectionate toward _____ owner.
    A) its   B) it's

_____ 3. A person who has a dog must care for _____ needs.
    A) its   B) it's

_____ 4. If _____ well taken care of, a dog can be a good pet.
    A) its   B) it's

_____ 5. Both the owner and the dog may feel _____ part of the family!
    A) its   B) it's

Sound-Alikes *Its* and *It's*

Directions: Think about the meaning of each sentence. Decide if *its* or *it's* belongs in the blank. Write *A* or *B* on the line.

_____ 1. _____ been a long time since I rode a roller coaster.
    A) Its   B) It's

_____ 2. _____ hills look higher than they used to look.
    A) Its   B) It's

_____ 3. _____ tracks look a little shaky, don't you think?
    A) Its   B) It's

_____ 4. _____ not that I'm scared, you see . . .
    A) Its   B) It's

_____ 5. Oh, all right. I'll get in line. _____ going to be fun . . . right?
    A) Its   B) It's

Related materials for teaching Spelling: *Your* and *You're*

Reproducible: Pre-test and Post-test (page 18); Practice Page (page 17)

Enrichment Activity (page 16)

Rule Book Template (page 6); Individual Record Sheet (page 95)

"Practice With a Purpose": Sound-Alikes *Your* and *You're* (pages 75-76)

Spelling: *Your* and *You're*

The ideas on these three pages follow the flow chart of suggested steps for teaching, reteaching, and testing presented on page 3 of this book.

STEP 1:
Motivation—All Yours

Introduce the skill by writing several sentences with *your* and *you're* purposely misused. Ask students if they have ever written sentences like these and if they can tell what is wrong with them. Here are some suggested sentences:

- **Your** so lucky!
- Is this **you're** lucky day?
- What is **you're** secret?
- **Your** always the one who wins.
- I wish I had **you're** luck.
- I'm glad **your** a winner.

STEP 2:
Pre-test and Grouping for Instruction

It is probable that some of your students have interchanged *your* and *you're* in one of the ways illustrated in these sentences. Follow this brief oral introduction by giving all students the written pre-test (page 18). Record (or have students record) their scores on an individual record sheet (page 95). Sort through the record sheets and remove the tests of students who scored 100%. You may choose to give these students the post-test right away to verify mastery or wait to give it to them with the rest of the class. Form a group of students who scored 80% or lower for direct instruction and practice.

STEP 3:
Instruction

Present students with the sentences used in the motivational activity or other examples with similar misspellings of *your* and *you're*. Generate a rule for choosing the spelling *your* and one for *you're* by comparing each incorrect sentence with its correct counterpart. (If you are using the "Practice With a Purpose" coordinated mini-charts, use the rule page for this lesson.) The guidelines that follow differentiate the two words by intended meaning.

RULE 1  **Your means *belongs to you.***

Your shoes

Your shows ownership.

• Here are **your** shoes. (The shoes belong to you.)
• **Your** hair looks nice today. (The hair belongs to you.)

RULE 2 **You're means *you are.***

The *'re* in *you're* is short for *are.*
They're is a contraction for *they are.*

• **You're** my friend. (You are my friend.)
• I see that **you're** tired. (I see that you are tired.)

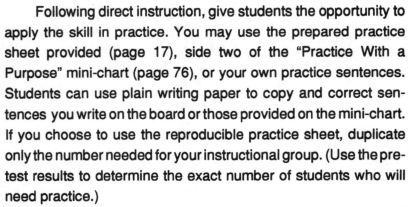

After presenting and discussing the rules above, help students correct the sentences given in the motivational activity by applying the rules.

✗ **Your** so lucky!
✓ **You're** so lucky! (you are)

✗ Is this **you're** lucky day?
✓ Is this **your** lucky day? (belongs to you)

✗ What is **you're** secret?
✓ What is **your** secret? (bleongs to you)

✗ **Your** always the one who wins.
✓ **You're** always the one who wins. (you are)

✗ I wish I had **you're** luck.
✓ I wish I had **your** luck. (belongs to you)

✗ I'm glad **your** a winner.
✓ I'm glad **you're** a winner. (you are)

You're tired!

STEP 4:
Apply and Practice

Following direct instruction, give students the opportunity to apply the skill in practice. You may use the prepared practice sheet provided (page 17), side two of the "Practice With a Purpose" mini-chart (page 76), or your own practice sentences. Students can use plain writing paper to copy and correct sentences you write on the board or those provided on the mini-chart. If you choose to use the reproducible practice sheet, duplicate only the number needed for your instructional group. (Use the pre-test results to determine the exact number of students who will need practice.)

Practice may be guided or done independently. Students may work individually, in pairs, or as a group. Correct the page together or privately to assess the need for reteaching before giving the post-test.

STEP 5:
Post-test and Reteaching

When your students have had sufficient instruction and practice, give the post-test. After recording scores on the individual record sheets, once again separate the sheets of those students who scored 80% or less on the post-test for reteaching. You may use or reuse any of the materials suggested in Step 4 for reteaching.

Follow-up / Enrichment

Once students have mastered the skill, make certain they retain it by giving a follow-up activity several weeks later. An excellent way to do this is to see if they can identify errors and use the skill in context. Below is a short story you can copy onto chart paper to check for retention. Have students supply *your* or *you're* in each blank. Or, if you prefer, use the prepared reproducible activity sheet on the following page. **Tip!** Let any students who have tried (or would like to try) skiing share their impressions of the experience.

To be corrected

It's Downhill From Here

_____toes are like ice. That clicking is the sound of _____ teeth chattering. _____ legs are as stiff as boards and _____ soaked to the bone. Even _____ hair is caked with snow. But I can't understand why _____ hanging onto that tree.

What's the matter? Aren't you enjoying _____ first ski trip?

Corrected

It's Downhill From Here

<u>**Your**</u> toes are like ice. That clicking is the sound of <u>**your**</u> teeth chattering. <u>**Your**</u> legs are as stiffs as boards and <u>**you're**</u> soaked to the bone. Even <u>**your**</u> hair is caked with snow. But I can't understand why <u>**you're**</u> hanging onto that tree.

What's the matter? Aren't you enjoying <u>**your**</u> first ski trip?

ANSWER KEYS

Pre-test:

1. B) You're
2. A) your
3. A) your
4. B) You're
5. B) you're

Practice:

1. A) Your
2. B) You're
3. B) you're
4. A) your
5. A) your
6. B) You're
7. A) your
8. B) you're
9. B) You're
10. A) your

Post-test:

1. B) You're
2. B) You're
3. A) your
4. A) Your
5. B) you're

**Practice With a Purpose—
Sound-Alikes *Your* and *You're***

1. You're 2. your 3. your 4. your 5. you're

Spelling *Your* and *You're*

Read the story. Use the rules you have learned about *your* and *you're* to decide which spelling belongs in each blank. Then copy the story completed correctly on the lines below.

**It's Downhill
From Here**

____ toes are like ice. That

clicking is the sound of ____ teeth

chattering. ____ legs are as stiff as

boards and ____ soaked to the bone.

Even ____ hair is caked with snow. But I

can't understand why ____ hanging onto that tree!

What's the matter? Aren't you enjoying ____ first ski trip?

_____

_____

_____

_____

_____

_____

_____

_____

Sound-Alikes *Your* and *You're*

Directions: Read carefully. Decide if *your* or *you're* belongs in the blank. Circle *A* or *B*.

A Special Invitation

A) Your   B) You're   1. _____ friend Jean called.

A) Your   B) You're   2. _____ invited to a special party.

A) your   B) you're   3. She'd like to know if _____ coming.

A) your   B) you're   4. She invited everyone who went on _____ trip last year.

A) your   B) you're   5. I guess _____ old shoes won't do for this party.

A) Your   B) You're   6. _____ going to need a gift, too.

A) your   B) you're   7. Let's go to _____ favorite store.

A) your   B) you're   8. We can go whenever _____ ready.

A) Your   B) You're   9. Oh, wait. _____ supposed to call Jean back.

A) your   B) you're   10. First, let's check the mail to see if _____ invitation came.

Name _____ **Date** _____ **Score** _____

Sound-Alikes *Your* and *You're*

Directions: Read carefully. Decide if *your* or *you're* belongs in the blank. Circle *A* or *B*.

A) Your   B) You're   1. _____ a good tennis player.

A) your   B) you're   2. I like _____ backhand.

A) your   B) you're   3. Where did you get _____ racket?

A) Your   B) You're   4. _____ playing Scott next, right?

A) your   B) you're   5. I hope _____ the winner!

Name _____ **Date** _____ **Score** _____

Sound-Alikes *Your* and *You're*

Directions: Read carefully. Decide if *your* or *you're* belongs in the blank. Circle *A* or *B*.

A) Your   B) You're   1. _____ the president.

A) Your   B) You're   2. _____ about to give a speech.

A) your   B) you're   3. Suddenly you realize that you're still in _____ pajamas!

A) Your   B) You're   4. _____ face turns bright red.

A) your   B) you're   5. Good thing _____ dreaming!

18

Related materials for teaching Spelling: *Whose* and *Who's*
Reproducible: Pre-test and Post-test (page 24); Practice Page (page 23)
Enrichment Activity (page 22)
Rule Book Template (page 6); Individual Record Sheet (page 95)
"Practice With a Purpose": Sound-Alikes *Whose* and *Who's* (pages 77-78)

Spelling: *Whose* and *Who's*

The ideas on these three pages follow the flow chart of suggested steps for teaching, reteaching, and testing presented on page 3 of this book.

Who?

STEP 1:
Motivation—Who's There?

Introduce the skill by having students write this "knock, knock" joke: *Knock, knock. Who's there? Who. Who who? The owl whose line you just stole!* Write it correctly on the board and have students underline the words *who's* and *whose*. Challenge students to state the difference between the two words. Next, write several sentences with *whose* and *who's* purposely misspelled in some cases. Ask students if they can find the ones with errors. Here are some suggested sentences:

- **Whose** there?
- I don't know **whose** pen I borrowed. *(correct)*
- **Who's** been to a football game? *(correct)*
- **Who's** absent today? *(correct)*
- It's the person **who's** paper is missing.
- I'm the one **whose** bringing dessert.

STEP 2:
Pre-test and Grouping for Instruction

It is probable that some of your students have interchanged *whose* and *who's* sometime in their writing. Follow the introduction by giving all students the written pre-test (page 24). Record (or have students record) their scores on an individual record sheet (page 95). Sort through the record sheets and remove the tests of students who scored 100%. You may choose to give these students the post-test right away to verify mastery or wait to give it to them with the rest of the class. Form a group of students who scored 80% or lower for direct instruction and practice.

STEP 3:
Instruction

Present students with the sentences used in the motivational activity or other examples with similar uses of *whose* and *who's*. Generate a rule for choosing the spelling *whose* and one for *who's* by comparing each incorrect sentence with its correct counterpart. The words are differentiated by intended meaning. (If you are using "Practice With a Purpose" coordinated mini-charts, use the rule page for this lesson.) Two rules that cover most uses of *whose* and *who's* are these:

RULE 1 ☞ *Whose* **means** *belongs to whom*.

Whose shows ownership.

• **Whose** book is this? (belongs to whom)

RULE 2 ☞ *Who's* **means** *who is* **or** *who has*.

The *'s* in *who's* is short for *is* or *has*.
Who's is a contraction for *who is* or *who has*.

• **Who's** here? (who is)
• **Who's** been here? (who has)

After presenting and discussing the rules above, help students apply the rules to correct the sentences given in the motivational activity.

✓ **Who's** there? NOT ✗ **Whose** there? (who is)
✓ I don't know **whose** pen I borrowed. CORRECT (belongs to whom)
✓ **Who's** been to a football game? CORRECT (who has)
✓ **Who's** absent today? CORRECT (who is)
✓ It's the person **whose** paper is missing. NOT ✗ . . . **who's** paper . . . (belongs to whom)
✓ I'm the one **who's** bringing dessert. NOT ✗ . . . **whose** bringing . . . (who is)

STEP 4:
Apply and Practice

Following direct instruction, give students the opportunity to apply the skill in practice. You may use the prepared practice sheet provided (page 23), side two of the "Practice With a Purpose" mini-chart (page 78), or your own practice sentences. Students can use plain writing paper to copy and correct sentences you write on the board or those provided on the mini-chart. If you choose to use the reproducible practice sheet, duplicate only the number needed for your instructional group. (Use the pre-test results to determine the exact number of students who will need practice.)

Practice may be guided or done independently. Students may work individually, in pairs, or as a group. Correct the page together or privately to assess the need for reteaching before giving the post-test.

STEP 5:
Post-test and Reteaching

When your students have had sufficient instruction and practice, give the post-test. After recording scores on the individual record sheets, once again separate the sheets of those students who scored 80% or less on the post-test for reteaching. You may use or reuse any of the materials suggested in Step 4 for reteaching.

Follow-up / Enrichment

Once students have mastered the skill, make certain they retain it by giving a follow-up activity several weeks later. An excellent way to do this is to see if they can apply the skill in context. At the above right is a story you can copy onto chart paper to check for retention. Have students fill in the blanks with *whose* or *who's*. Or, if you prefer, use the prepared reproducible activity sheet on the following page. **Tip!** Have students explain their choices based on the intended meanings.

To be corrected

Who's New?

"____ that guy, Rosa?" asked Abby.

"He's the one ___ new at school. He just moved here from Texas," said Rosa.

"I wonder ___ going to show him around."

"Hmm. Do I detect someone ____ plan it is to do the job herself?" asked Rosa.

"Well, anyone ___ ever been new at school knows it can be confusing. I'm sure he'd like to make a friend—especially one ___ been in this situation."

"You're right. Let's be the ones ___ friendliness makes him feel right at home!"

Corrected

Who's New?

"**Who's** that guy, Rosa?" asked Abby.

"He's the one **who's** new at school. He just moved here from Texas," said Rosa.

"I wonder **who's** going to show him around."

"Hmm. Do I detect someone **whose** plan it is to do the job herself?" asked Rosa.

"Well, anyone **who's** ever been new at school knows it can be confusing. I'm sure he'd like to make a friend—especially one **who's** been in this situation."

"You're right. Let's be the ones **whose** friendliness makes him feel right at home!"

ANSWER KEYS

Pre-test:	Practice:		Post-test:
1. B) Who's	1. A) whose	6. A) whose	1. A) whose
2. B) who's	2. B) who's	7. B) who's	2. B) who's
3. B) Who's	3. B) who's	8. A) whose	3. A) whose
4. A) whose	4. A) whose	9. B) who's	4. B) who's
5. A) whose	5. A) whose	10. A) whose	5. B) who's

Practice With a Purpose—		
Sound-Alikes *Whose* and *Who's*	1. who's	4. whose
	2. who's	5. who's
	3. who's	

Spelling *Whose* and *Who's*

Read the story. Use the rules you have learned about *whose* and *who's* to decide which spelling belongs in each blank. Then copy the story completed correctly on the lines below.

Who's New?

"___ that guy, Rosa?" asked Abby.

"He's the one ___ new at school. He just moved here from Texas," said Rosa.

"I wonder ___ going to show him around."

"Hmm. Do I detect someone ___ plan it is to do the job herself?" asked Rosa.

"Well, anyone ___ ever been new at school knows it can be confusing. I'm sure he'd like to make a friend—especially one ___ been in this situation."

"You're right. Let's be the ones ___ friendliness makes him feel right at home!"

_____

_____

_____

_____

_____

_____

_____

_____

_____

_____

_____

_____

_____

Sound-Alikes *Whose* and *Who's*

Directions: Read carefully. If *whose* belongs in the blank, write *A* on the line. If *who's* belongs in the blank, write *B* on the line.

Who Is . . .?
Can you identify each famous Who's Who? Check your answers below.

_____ 1. The president _____ assassination shocked the world
A) whose   B) who's

_____ 2. The man _____ credited with inventing the light bulb
A) whose   B) who's

_____ 3. The only woman _____ served on the U.S. Supreme Court
A) whose   B) who's

_____ 4. The star of a movie _____ most famous line is "Phone home"
A) whose   B) who's

_____ 5. The astronaut _____ footprint was the first on the moon
A) whose   B) who's

_____ 6. The Nobel Prize winner _____ dream of equal rights for people
of all colors did not end with his assassination
A) whose   B) who's

_____ 7. The woman who attempted to fly solo around the world and _____
never been found
A) whose   B) who's

_____ 8. The pop rock star _____ symbol is a single white glove
A) whose   B) who's

_____ 9. The man _____ credited with the discovery of the polio vaccine
A) whose   B) who's

_____ 10. The U.S. president after _____ name the "teddy" bear was fashioned
A) whose   B) who's

Answers: *1) John F. Kennedy 2) Thomas Edison 3) Sandra Day O'Connor 4) ET 5) Neil Armstrong
6) Martin Luther King, Jr. 7) Amelia Earhart 8) Michael Jackson 9) Jonas Salk 10) Theodore "Teddy" Roosevelt*

Name _____ **Date** _____ **Score** _____

Sound-Alikes *Whose* and *Who's*

Directions: Read carefully. If *whose* belongs in the blank, write *A* on the line. If *who's* belongs in the blank, write *B* on the line.

_____ 1. Knock, knock. "_____ there?"
A) Whose   B) Who's

_____ 2. "Pizza delivery for someone _____ ordered a large pepperoni."
A) whose   B) who's

_____ 3. "_____ going to pay?" joked Dad.
A) Whose   B) Who's

_____ 4. "The one _____ wallet is full, Dad," laughed Tim.
A) whose   B) who's

_____ 5. "OK, but I know _____ stomach will end up full," said Dad.
A) whose   B) who's

Name _____ **Date** _____ **Score** _____

Sound-Alikes *Whose* and *Who's*

Directions: Read carefully. If *whose* belongs in the blank, write *A* on the line. If *who's* belongs in the blank, write *B* on the line.

_____ 1. "For _____ team are you rooting?" asked Lynn.
A) whose   B) who's

_____ 2. "The one _____ winning, of course," answered Shannon.
A) whose   B) who's

_____ 3. "Did you see _____ number was on the jersey of the kicker?"
A) whose   B) who's

_____ 4. "I think it is Dave _____ wearing number seven," said Lynn.
A) whose   B) who's

_____ 5. "He's the one _____ kicked eight field goals already this season!"
A) whose   B) who's

Related materials for teaching Spelling: *There,* *Their,* **and** *They're*
Reproducible: Pre-test and Post-test (page 30); Practice Page (page 29)
Enrichment Activity (page 28)
Rule Book Template (page 6); Individual Record Sheet (page 95)
"Practice With a Purpose": Sound-Alikes *There, Their,* and *They're* (pages 79-80)

Spelling: *There, Their,* and *They're*

The ideas on these three pages follow the flow chart of suggested steps for teaching, reteaching, and testing presented on page 3 of this book.

STEP 1:
Motivation—They're There

Introduce the skill by writing several sentences using *there, their,* and *they're* correctly. Ask students to think about the meaning of the word in each sentence. Here are some suggestions:

(there)	*(their)*	*(they're)*
• Are you going **there**?	• Do you know **their** names?	• I know **they're** coming.
• **There** is my lost hat!	• **Their** house was just painted.	• **They're** good sports.

STEP 2:
Pre-test and Grouping for Instruction

To check students' proficiency at recognizing the correct spelling of *there, their,* and *they're* in context, give all students the written pre-test (page 30). Record (or have students record) their scores on an individual record sheet (page 95). Sort through the record sheets and remove the tests of students who scored 100%. You may choose to give these students the post-test right away to verify mastery or wait to give it to them with the rest of the class. Form a group of students who scored 80% or lower for direct instruction and practice.

STEP 3:
Instruction

Present students with the sentences used in the motivational activity, two at a time. Begin by discussing the meaning of the word *there* in the first two sentences. Have students suggest a rule for the spelling *there.* An easy rule to remember is this:

RULE 1   *There* **tells** *where.*

 If *there* answers the question *where,* use the *-ere* spelling. *There* and *where* both end with *-ere!*

• Are you going **there**? (Where? There!)
• **There** is my lost hat. (Where? There!)

Continue with the next two sentences. Discuss the meaning of the word *their* in each. Have students create a rule for the spelling *their*. An easy rule to remember is this:

RULE 2   *Their* means *belongs to them*.

Their shows ownership.

- Do you know **their** names? (belongs to them)
- **Their** house was just painted. (belongs to them)

Finally, present the last pair of sentences. Discuss the meaning of the word *they're* in each. Have students create a rule for the spelling *they're*. An easy rule to remember is this:

RULE 3   *They're* means *they are*.

The *-re* in *they're* is short for *are*. *They're* is a contraction for *they are*.

- I know **they're** coming. (they are)
- **They're** good sports. (they are)

Once you have gone over the six motivational sentences above, review the rules and provide practice in differentiating among *there, their,* and *they're*. (If you are using "Practice With a Purpose" coordinated mini-charts, use the rule page for review.)

STEP 4:
Apply and Practice

Following direct instruction, give students the opportunity to apply the skill in practice. You may use the prepared practice sheet provided (page 29), side two of the "Practice With a Purpose" mini-chart (page 80), or your own practice sentences. Students can use plain writing paper to copy and correct sentences you write on the board or those provided on the mini-chart. If you choose to use the reproducible practice sheet, duplicate only the number needed for your instructional group. (Use the pre-test results to determine the exact number of students who will need practice.)

Practice may be guided or done independently. Students may work individually, in pairs, or as a group. Correct the page together or privately to assess the need for reteaching before giving the post-test.

Their house

STEP 5:
Post-test and Reteaching

When your students have had sufficient instruction and practice, give the post-test. After recording scores on the individual record sheets, once again separate the sheets of those students who scored 80% or less on the post-test for reteaching. You may use or reuse any of the materials suggested in Step 4 for reteaching.

Follow-up / Enrichment

Once students have mastered the skill, make certain they retain it by giving a follow-up activity several weeks later. An excellent way to do this is to see if they can apply the skill in context. Below is a poem you can copy onto chart paper or a duplicating master to check for retention. Have students fill in *there, their,* or *they're* in each blank. Or, if you prefer, use the prepared reproducible activity sheet on the following page. **Tip!** Invite students to write their own poems about animals they would like to observe in their natural habitats.

To be corrected	*Corrected*

Cool!

The Arctic's cool. Have you been ___?
___ are walruses and polar bears.
___ grunts and groans are mean and loud.
They try to scare you with ___ sound.
But ___ really more afraid of you,
And why you're ___ and what you'll do.
So if you ever travel ___,
You can watch and even stare.
But don't you ever make a fuss—
'Cause ___ the ones afraid of us!

Cool!

The Arctic's cool. Have you been **there**?
There are walruses and polar bears.
Their grunts and groans are mean and loud.
They try to scare you with **their** sound.
But **they're** really more afraid of you,
And why you're **there** and what you'll do.
So if you ever travel **there**,
You can watch and even stare.
But don't you ever make a fuss—
'Cause **they're** the ones afraid of us!

ANSWER KEYS

Pre-test:

1. A) there
2. A) there
3. B) their
4. B) Their
5. C) They're

Practice:

1. B) their
2. C) They're
3. C) they're
4. A) There
5. B) their
6. B) their
7. B) their
8. A) There
9. A) there
10. C) They're

Post-test:

1. A) There
2. B) their
3. C) They're
4. A) there
5. B) Their

Practice With a Purpose—
Sound-Alikes *There, Their,* and *They're*

1. They're   2. their   3. there   4. Their   5. there

Spelling *There*, *Their*, and *They're*

Read the poem. Use the rules you have learned about *there, their,* and *they're* to decide which spelling belongs in each blank. Then copy the poem completed correctly on the lines below.

Cool!

The Arctic's cool! Have you been ____?

____ are walruses and polar bears.

____ grunts and groans are mean and loud.

They try to scare you with ____ sound.

But ____ really more afraid of you,

And why you're ____ and what you'll do.

So if you ever travel ____,

You can watch and even stare.

But don't you ever make a fuss—

'Cause ____ the ones afraid of us!

_____

_____

_____

_____

_____

_____

_____

_____

_____

_____

28

Sound-Alikes *There, Their,* and *They're*

Directions: Decide which word belongs in the blank: *there, their,* or *they're.* Write *A*, *B*, or *C* on the line.

Alignators and Crocodiles

_____ 1. Alligators and crocodiles both have long, low bodies and use _____ powerful jaws to eat animals that come near the water.
A) there   B) their   C) they're

_____ 2. _____ both large reptiles.
A) There   B) Their   C) They're

_____ 3. Alligators and crocodiles may seem alike, but _____ different!
A) there   B) their   C) they're

_____ 4. _____ are several important differences between them.
A) There   B) Their   C) They're

_____ 5. For example, _____ heads are shaped differently.
A) there   B) their   C) they're

_____ 6. Alligators' heads are more rounded, and only _____ upper teeth show when their mouths are closed.
A) there   B) their   C) they're

_____ 7. Crocodiles' faces are more pointed and _____ fourth tooth on the lower jaw shows when their mouths are closed.
A) there   B) their   C) they're

_____ 8. _____ are differences in size, too. Alligators are smaller than crocodiles.
A) There   B) Their   C) They're

_____ 9. Did you know that _____ are only two places to find alligators—in the swamps of the southern United States and in a small area of China?
A) there   B) their   C) they're

_____10. Crocodiles, however, live in warm waters throughout the world. _____ not only more plentiful than alligators, but also more dangerous to people.
A) There   B) Their   C) They're

Name _____ **Date** _____ **Score** _____

Sound-Alikes *There, Their,* and *They're*

Directions: Decide which word belongs in the blank: *there, their,* or *they're*. Write *A, B,* or *C* on the line.

_____ 1. At night _____ are many lights in the sky.
     A) there   B) their   C) they're

_____ 2. Most are from stars, but _____ are also lights from planets.
     A) there   B) their   C) they're

_____ 3. Planets give off no light of _____ own.
     A) there   B) their   C) they're

_____ 4. _____ light comes from reflection from the sun.
     A) There   B) Their   C) They're

_____ 5. _____ sometimes brighter than the stars.
     A) There   B) Their   C) They're

Name _____ **Date** _____ **Score** _____

Sound-Alikes *There, Their,* and *They're*

Directions: Decide which word belongs in the blank: *there, their,* or *they're*. Write *A, B,* or *C* on the line.

_____ 1. _____ is a big sale at King's department store.
     A) There   B) Their   C) They're

_____ 2. I saw _____ ad in the newspaper.
     A) there   B) their   C) they're

_____ 3. _____ advertising jeans at 30% off!
     A) There   B) Their   C) They're

_____ 4. I'm going _____ right away to get some.
     A) there   B) their   C) they're

_____ 5. _____ sale only lasts until 8:00 tonight!
     A) There   B) Their   C) They're

Related materials for teaching Spelling: *To, Two*, and *Too*
Reproducible: Pre-test and Post-test (page 36); Practice Page (page 35)
Enrichment Activity (page 34)
Rule Book Template (page 6); Individual Record Sheet (page 95)
"Practice With a Purpose": Sound-Alikes *To, Two*, and *Too* (pages 81-82)

Spelling: *To, Two*, and *Too*

The ideas on these three pages follow the flow chart of suggested steps for teaching, reteaching, and testing presented on page 3 of this book.

STEP 1:
Motivation—What to Do?

Introduce the skill by writing several sentences with *to, two,* and *too* purposely misspelled in some cases. Challenge students to find the ones with errors. Here are some suggested sentences:

- I don't know what **too** do.
- She had **to** chances.
- It ran **too** fast. *(correct)*
- I like pizza, **to**.
- Bring the ball **to** me. *(correct)*
- This dress is **two** short.

STEP 2:
Pre-test and Grouping for Instruction

Find out your students' proficiency at recognizing the correct spelling of *to, two,* and *two* by giving all students the written pre-test (page 36). Record (or have students record) their scores on an individual record sheet (page 95). Sort through the record sheets and remove the tests of students who scored 100%. You may choose to give these students the post-test right away to verify mastery or wait to give it to them with the rest of the class. Form a group of students who scored 80% or lower for direct instruction and practice.

STEP 3:
Instruction

Present students with the same sentences used in the motivational activity or other examples with similar uses of *to, two,* and *too.* (If you are using the "Practice With a Purpose" coordinated mini-charts, use the rule page for this lesson.) Guide students toward discovering that the differences among the three spellings relate to intended meaning. Compare each incorrect sentence with its correct counterpart. An easy-to-remember rule for using each spelling form—*to, two,* and *too*—appears on the next page.

RULE 1  **To** means *move toward* or is part of a verb (action).

- Go **to** the table. (*to* shows direction—move toward)
- The officer told them **to** stop. (*to* is part of the action *stop*)

RULE 2 **Two** is the word for the number 2.

- The team scored **two** goals. (2)
- That is **two** more than last time! (2)

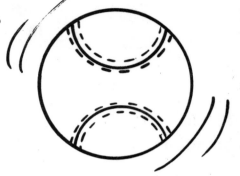

RULE 3 **Too** means *also* or *excess*.

- Bears like honey and I do, **too**. (also)
- It is **too** hot today. (excess)

I like to eat pizza.
My favorite two toppings are
pepperoni and mushroom.
Do you like those, too?

✗ I don't know what **too** do.
(*To* is part of a verb: I don't know what **to** do.)

✗ She had **to** chances.
(*Two* means the number 2: She had **two** chances.)

✓ It ran **too** fast.
(*Too* means excess: correct as is)

✗ I like pizza, **to**.
(*Too* means also: I like pizza, **too**.)

✓ Bring the ball **to** me.
(*To* means move toward: correct as is)

✗ This dress is **two** short.
(*Too* means excess: This dress is **too** short.)

STEP 4:
Apply and Practice

Following direct instruction, give students the opportunity to apply the skill in practice. You may use the prepared practice sheet provided (page 35), side two of the "Practice With a Purpose" mini-chart (page 82), or your own practice sentences. Students can use plain writing paper to copy and correct sentences you write on the board or those provided on the mini-chart. If you choose to use the reproducible practice sheet, duplicate only the number needed for your instructional group. (Use the pre-test results to determine the exact number of students who will need practice.)

Practice may be guided or done independently. Students may work individually, in pairs, or as a group. Correct the page together or privately to assess the need for reteaching before giving the post-test.

STEP 5:
Post-test and Reteaching

When your students have had sufficient instruction and practice, give the post-test. After recording scores on the individual record sheets, once again separate the sheets of those students who scored 80% or less on the post-test for reteaching. You may use or reuse any of the materials suggested in Step 4 for reteaching.

Follow-up / Enrichment

Once students have mastered the skill, make certain they retain it by giving a follow-up activity several weeks later. An excellent way to do this is to see if they can correctly use the skill in context. Copy the story onto chart paper to check for retention. Or, if you prefer, use the prepared reproducible activity sheet on the following page. Have students complete the passage by filling in *to, two,* or *too* in each blank. **Tip!** Invite students to find out more about the Bermuda Triangle.

To be corrected

The Bermuda Triangle
In an area off the southeastern United States lies a triangular space of ocean known ___ the world as the Bermuda Triangle.

Its claim ___ fame is the high number of mysterious disappearances of planes and ships in this area. Many seem simply __ vanish! This has happened not only in bad weather, but in good weather, ___. Even with perfectly operating ___-way radio contact, travelers have disappeared.

Whatever the cause, there are simply ___ many occurrences to dismiss the problem as coincidence. Yet no one so far has been able ___ explain this strange phenomenon.

Corrected

The Bermuda Triangle
In an area off the southeastern United States lies a triangular space of ocean known **to** the world as the Bermuda Triangle.

Its claim **to** fame is the high number of mysterious disappearances of planes and ships in this area. Many seem simply **to** vanish! This has happened not only in bad weather, but in good weather, **too**. Even with perfectly operating **two**-way radio contact, travelers have disappeared.

Whatever the cause, there are simply **too** many occurrences to dismiss the problem as coincidence. Yet no one so far has been able **to** explain this strange phenomenon.

ANSWER KEYS

Pre-test:	Practice:		Post-test:
1. A) to	1. A) to	6. C) too	1. B) two
2. B) two	2. B) two	7. C) too	2. A) to
3. C) too	3. B) two	8. A) to	3. C) too
4. A) to	4. C) too	9. A) to	4. A) to
5. C) too	5. A) to	10. C) too	5. C) too

Practice With a Purpose—
Sound-Alikes *To, Two,* and *Too*

1. ~~too~~ to   4. ~~two~~ too
2. ~~two~~ too   5. ~~to~~ too
3. ~~Too~~ Two

Spelling *To, Two,* and *Too*

Read the story. Use the rules you have learned about *to, two,* and *too* to decide which spelling belongs in each blank. Then copy the story completed correctly on the lines below.

New York

Bermuda

Miami

The Bermuda Triangle

In an area off the southeastern United States lies a triangular space of ocean known ___ the world as the Bermuda Triangle.

Its claim ___ fame is the high number of mysterious disappearances of planes and ships in this area. Many seem simply ___ vanish! This has happened not only in bad weather, but in good weather, ___. Even with perfectly operating ___-way radio contact, travelers have disappeared.

Whatever the cause, there are simply ___ many occurrences to dismiss the problem as coincidence. Yet no one so far has been able ___ explain this strange phenomenon.

_____

_____

_____

_____

_____

_____

_____

_____

_____

_____

_____

_____

_____

_____

Sound-Alikes *To, Two,* and *Too*

Directions: Read carefully. Decide which word belongs in the blank: *to, two,* or *too.* Circle *A, B,* or *C* in the answer box.

ANSWER BOX		
to	*two*	*too*
1. A	B	C
2. A	B	C
3. A	B	C
4. A	B	C
5. A	B	C
6. A	B	C
7. A	B	C
8. A	B	C
9. A	B	C
10. A	B	C

Crazy Critter

It would be fun (1)_____ create a crazy imaginary animal. I would start by having it have the body of an elephant, but only (2)_____ legs. I think I would give it (3)_____ tails, (4) _____!

My critter would have (5)_____ have a long neck, but not (6)_____ long! The neck of a horse would do.

I would have its head look like a monkey's, and its ears be furry, (7)_____. I would give it a big cowbell (8)_____ wear around its neck so it could not sneak up on you!

Finally, I would have (9)_____ give it a name— MONKEYFANT. Why don't you create a Crazy Critter, (10) _____?

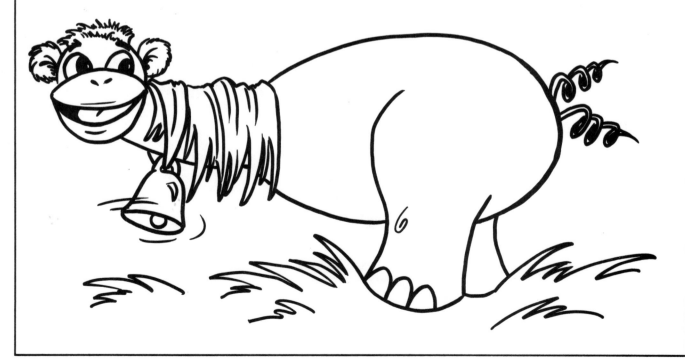

Pre-test

Name _____ Date _____ Score _____

Sound-Alikes *To, Two,* and *Too*

Directions: Read carefully. Decide which word belongs in the blank: *to, two,* or *too*. Circle *A*, *B*, or *C* in the answer box.

I have a big project (1)___ do! The assignment is to write about (2)___ inventors. I have to include pictures of their inventions, (3)___. I guess I had better get (4)___ the library before it is (5)___ late!

ANSWER BOX

	to	*two*	*too*
1.	A	B	C
2.	A	B	C
3.	A	B	C
4.	A	B	C
5.	A	B	C

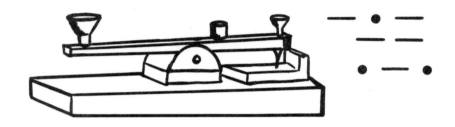

Post-test

Name _____ Date _____ Score _____

Sound-Alikes *To, Two,* and *Too*

Directions: Read carefully. Decide which word belongs in the blank: *to, two,* or *too*. Circle *A*, *B*, or *C* in the answer box.

I have to be ready to go soon. I have (1)___ friends coming by (2)___ pick me up. We are stopping at another friend's house, (3)___. We have (4)___ make it to the movie theater by 6:45 or it will be (5)___ late to get in.

ANSWER BOX

	to	*two*	*too*
1.	A	B	C
2.	A	B	C
3.	A	B	C
4.	A	B	C
5.	A	B	C

ADMIT ONE
Carnival Theater
7:00 PM SHOW

Related materials for teaching Spelling: Plurals—Adding -es
Reproducible: Pre-test and Post-test (page 42); Practice Page (page 41)
Enrichment Activity (page 40)
Rule Book Template (page 6); Individual Record Sheet (page 95)
"Practice With a Purpose": Plurals—Adding -es (pages 83-84)

Spelling: Plurals—Adding -es

The ideas on these three pages follow the flow chart of suggested steps
for teaching, reteaching, and testing presented on page 3 of this book.

STEP 1:
Motivation—Making Wishes

Introduce this spelling skill by writing sample sentences containing misspellings of plurals whose singular form ends in -s, -x, -sh, or -ch. Ask students to find the misspelled words. As they do, underline the key ending (-s, -x, -sh, -ch) in the word. Here are some suggested sentences:

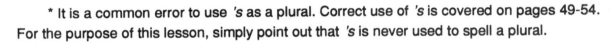

(s) • We have new **dresses's.***   *(sh)* • You get three **wishs**.

    • They ride different **buss**.   • Are those new **dishs**?

(x) • These are your **boxs**.   *(ch)* • The **branchs** are bending.

    • Some **foxs** are red.   • I grew two **inchs**.

    * It is a common error to use *'s* as a plural. Correct use of *'s* is covered on pages 49-54. For the purpose of this lesson, simply point out that *'s* is never used to spell a plural.

STEP 2:
Pre-test and Grouping for Instruction

Check students' recognition of plurals made by adding *-es* to words ending in *-s, -x, -sh,* or *-ch* by giving them the written pre-test (page 42). Record (or have students record) their scores on an individual record sheet (page 95). Sort through the record sheets and remove the tests of students who scored 100%. You may choose to give these students the post-test right away to verify mastery or wait to give it to them with the rest of the class. Form a group of students who scored 80% or lower for direct instruction and practice.

STEP 3:
Instruction

If necessary, review the meaning of the word *plural* (more than one). Remind students that most plurals are formed simply by adding *-s* to the word, but there are exceptions. To help students recognize and avoid misspelling of those plurals formed by adding *-es* to words ending in *-s, -x, -sh,* or *-ch,* begin by correcting together the sentences in the motivational activity. Prepare a chart like the one on the following page and, as you work through the sentences, add appropriate words to each category. Challenge students to suggest more examples and a general rule for spelling these types of plurals.

The rule below covers most cases for forming plurals of words ending in *-s, -x, -sh,* or *-ch* by adding *-es.* (If you are using "Practice With a Purpose" coordinated mini-charts, use the rule page for this lesson.)

	ONE (singular)		MORE (plural)
-s	dress bu**s**	⇨	dresses buses
-x	bo**x** fo**x**	⇨	boxes foxes
-sh	wi**sh** di**sh**	⇨	wishes dishes
-ch	bran**ch** in**ch**	⇨	branches inches

RULE 1 **Add *-es* to words ending in *-s, -x, -sh,* or *-ch* to make them plural.**

✓ We have new **dresses**.
✓ They ride different **buses**.
✓ These are your **boxes**.
✓ Some **foxes** are red.
✓ You get three **wishes**.
✓ Are those new **dishes**?
✓ The **branches** are bending.
✓ I grew two **inches**.

Also **classes, axes, taxes, brushes, beaches, benches,** *and* **watches.**

STEP 4:
Apply and Practice

Following direct instruction, give students the opportunity to apply the skill in practice. You may use the prepared practice sheet provided (page 41), side two of the "Practice With a Purpose" mini-chart (page 84), or your own practice sentences. Students can use plain writing paper to copy and correct sentences you write on the board or those provided on the mini-chart. If you choose to use the reproducible practice sheet, duplicate only the number needed for your instructional group. (Use the pre-test results to determine the exact number of students who will need practice.)

Practice may be guided or done independently. Students may work individually, in pairs, or as a group. Correct the page together or privately to assess the need for reteaching before giving the post-test.

STEP 5:
Post-test and Reteaching

When your students have had sufficient instruction and practice, give the post-test. After recording scores on the individual record sheets, once again separate the sheets of those students who scored 80% or less on the post-test for reteaching. You may use or reuse any of the materials suggested in Step 4 for reteaching.

Follow-up / Enrichment

Once students have mastered the skill, make certain they retain it by giving a follow-up activity several weeks later. An excellent way to do this is to see if they can apply the skill in context. Below is a humorous poem you can copy onto chart paper to check for retention. Have students correct the errors. Or, if you prefer, use the prepared reproducible activity sheet on the following page. **Tip!** Invite students to write their own poem or story about a chore they dislike.

To be corrected

Out of the Kitchen
Don't leave me in this kitchen.
<u>Dishs</u> aren't my thing.
Instead of washing <u>glass's</u>
I'd do most anything.

I'd put away the <u>boxs</u>.
I'd vacuum and I'd dust.
I'd iron the pants and <u>dresses</u>
If you said I must.

I'd sew the holes with <u>stitchs</u>,
Tree <u>branchs</u> I would trim
To get out of this kitchen
And the mess it's in!

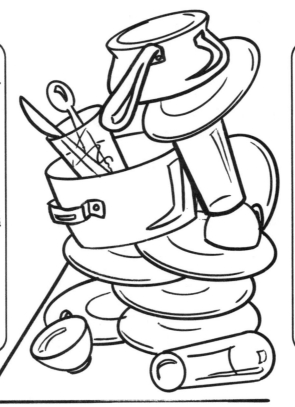

Corrected

Out of the Kitchen
Don't leave me in this kitchen.
<u>Dishes</u> aren't my thing.
Instead of washing **<u>glasses</u>**
I'd do most anything.

I'd put away the **<u>boxes</u>**.
I'd vacuum and I'd dust.
I'd iron the pants and <u>dresses</u>
If you said I must.

I'd sew the holes with **<u>stitches</u>**,
Tree **<u>branches</u>** I would trim
To get out of this kitchen
And the mess it's in!

ANSWER KEYS

Pre-test:
1. B) wishes
2. B) inches
3. B) taxes
4. A) nations
5. A) chances

Practice:
1. B) boxes
2. B) peaches
3. B) foxes
4. B) bunches
5. B) walruses
6. A) seeds
7. B) wishes
8. B) lunches
9. A) Fruits
10. A) beasts

Post-test:
1. B) axes
2. B) peaches
3. A) monkeys
4. B) dresses
5. B) brushes

**Practice With a Purpose—
Plurals—Adding *-es***

1. beaches
2. boxes
3. correct as is
4. wishes
5. sunglasses

Spelling Plurals—Adding *-es*

Read the poem. Use the rules you have learned about forming plurals of words ending in *-s, -x, -sh,* or *-ch* to decide if each underlined word is spelled correctly or incorrectly. Then copy the poem spelled correctly on the lines below.

Out of the Kitchen

Don't leave me in this kitchen.
<u>Dishs</u> aren't my thing.
Instead of washing <u>glass's</u>
I'd do most anything.

I'd put away the <u>boxs</u>.
I'd vacuum and I'd dust.
I'd iron the pants and <u>dresses</u>
If you said I must.

I'd sew the holes with <u>stitchs</u>,
Tree <u>branchs</u> I would trim
To get out of this kitchen
And the mess it's in!

Spelling Plurals—Adding *-es*

Directions: Read carefully. Circle the correct spelling of the plural form of the **boldfaced** word in each sentence.

Zoo Feast

A) boxs   B) boxes   1. Fifty **box** arrived at the zoo this morning.

A) peachs   B) peaches   2. One contained two dozen **peach**.

A) foxs   B) foxes   3. Another had some special treats for the **fox**.

A) bunchs   B) bunches   4. There were two crates filled with **bunch** of bananas.

A) walruss   B) walruses   5. There was even something for the **walrus**.

A) seeds   B) seedes   6. The birds would get 200 pounds of **seed**.

A) wishs   B) wishes   7. Had anything come to fulfill the **wish** of the lions?

A) lunchs   B) lunches   8. Yes, 12 crates of meat would be their **lunch**.

A) Fruits   B) Fruites   9. **Fruit** and vegetables filled 20 other containers.

A) beasts   B) beastes   10. There was something for everyone— a feast for the **beast**.

Spelling Plurals—Adding *-es*

Directions: Read carefully. Choose the correct spelling of the word that belongs in the blank. Circle *A* or *B*.

A) wish's   B) wishes   1. If you had four ____, what would they be?

A) inchs   B) inches   2. First, I would like to be two ____ taller.

A) taxs   B) taxes   3. Second, I would like there to be no more ____.

A) nations   B) nationes   4. For my third, I would choose peace for all ____.

A) chances   B) chance's   5. And last—this I choose most carefully—is for a hundred more ____ to change the first three.

✂

Spelling Plurals—Adding *-es*

Directions: Read carefully. Choose the correct spelling of the word pictured. Circle *A* or *B*.

1.

A. axs
B. axes

2.

A. peachs
B. peaches

3.

A. monkeys
B. monkeyes

4.

A. dress's
B. dresses

5.

A. brushs
B. brushes

FS-10171 Plain English—Spelling

Related materials for teaching Spelling: Plurals—Making Changes
Reproducible: Pre-test and Post-test (page 48); Practice Page (page 47)
Enrichment Activity (page 46)
Rule Book Template (page 6); Individual Record Sheet (page 95)
"Practice With a Purpose": Plurals—Making Changes (pages 85-86)

Spelling: Plurals—Making Changes

The ideas on these three pages follow the flow chart of suggested steps
for teaching, reteaching, and testing presented on page 3 of this book.

STEP 1:
Motivation—The Big Switch

Introduce the skill by writing several sentences containing plurals of words that end in *-f* or *-fe,* or with a consonant plus *-y.* Include correct and incorrect spellings. Challenge students to find the errors. Here are some suggested sentences:
- I will rake the **leafs**.
- Put the books on these **shelves**. *(correct)*
- These **knives** need sharpened. *(correct)*
- Does a cat really have nine **lifes**?
- I like birthday **parties**. *(correct)*
- Carla's **puppys** are really adorable.
- I read three **storys** about giants.

STEP 2:
Pre-test and Grouping for Instruction

Check students' recognition of plurals requiring the changing of *-f* or *-fe* to *-v* and *-y* to *-i* by giving all students the written pre-test (page 48). Record (or have students record) their scores on an individual record sheet (page 95). Sort through the record sheets and remove the tests of students who scored 100%. You may choose to give these students the post-test right away to verify mastery or wait to give it to them with the rest of the class. Form a group of students who scored 80% or lower for direct instruction and practice.

*Two **puppies** play in the **leaves**.*

STEP 3:
Instruction

If necessary, review the meaning of the word *plural* (more than one). Remind students that most plurals are formed by adding *-s* to the words, but there are exceptions. This lesson covers two cases in which letters are changed when forming plurals. To help students recognize and avoid misspelling of those plurals that require changing *-f* or *-fe* to *-v* and *-y* to *-i,* begin by correcting together the sentences in the motivational activity. Prepare two charts like the ones on the following page. Have students suggest two special rules that cover most cases of spelling plurals for words ending in *-f* or *-fe,* and consonant plus *-y.*

RULE 1 👉 To form the plural of most words that end in -*f* or -*fe*, change the -*f* or -*fe* to -*v* and add -*es*.

RULE 2 👉 To form the plural of words that end with a consonant and -*y*, change the -*y* to -*i* and add -*es*.

	ONE (singular)	MORE (plural)
-f, -fe	leaf	leaves
	shelf	shelves
	knife	knives
	life ⟹	lives
	scarf	scarves
	half	halves
	thief	thieves
	wolf	wolves

	ONE (singular)	MORE (plural)
C + y	puppy	puppies
	story	stories
	party	parties
	baby ⟹	babies
	lady	ladies
	butterfly	butterflies
	cherry	cherries
	pony	ponies

Have students explain why each sentence in the motivational activity is correct or incorrect. (If you are using "Practice With a Purpose" coordinated mini-charts, use the rule page for review.)

✗ I will rake the **leafs**. (Ends in -*f*, so apply Rule 1: **leaves**.)

✓ Put the books on these **shelves**. (Rule 1 was applied correctly.)

✓ These **knives** need sharpened. (Rule 1 was applied correctly.)

✗ Does a cat really have nine **lifes**? (Ends in -*fe*, so apply Rule 1: **lives**.)

✓ I like birthday **parties**. (Rule 2 was applied correctly.)

✗ Carla's **puppys** are really adorable. (Ends with a consonant + *y*, so apply Rule 2: **puppies**.)

✗ I read three **storys** about giants. (Ends with a consonant + *y*, so apply Rule 2: **stories**.)

STEP 4:
Apply and Practice

Following direct instruction, give students the opportunity to apply the skill in practice. You may use the prepared practice sheet provided (page 47), side two of the "Practice With a Purpose" mini-chart (page 86), or your own practice sentences. Students can use plain writing paper to copy and correct sentences you write on the board or those provided on the mini-chart. If you choose to use the reproducible practice sheet, duplicate only the number needed for your instructional group. (Use the pre-test results to determine the exact number of students who will need practice.)

Practice may be guided or done independently. Students may work individually, in pairs, or as a group. Correct the page together or privately to assess the need for reteaching before giving the post-test.

STEP 5:
Post-test and Reteaching

When your students have had sufficient instruction and practice, give the post-test. After recording scores on the individual record sheets, once again separate the sheets of those students who scored 80% or less on the post-test for reteaching. You may use or re-use any of the materials suggested in Step 4 for reteaching.

Follow-up / Enrichment

Once students have mastered the skill, make certain they retain it by giving a follow-up activity several weeks later. An excellent way to do this is to see if they can correctly use the skill in context. At the right is a poem you can copy onto chart paper to check for retention. Have students find and fix the spelling errors. Or, if you prefer, use the prepared reproducible activity sheet on the following page. **Tip!** Read the classic story "The Shoemaker and the Elves" to your students. Have older students retell their favorite childhood stories.

To be corrected

Little Shoemakers

Once there were some little elfs.
They made shoes for shoe store shelfs.
Their lifes were filled with pitter-patter.
Making shoes was all that mattered.

Everyone helped—even wifes and babys,
Making shoes for lords and ladys.
And when their day's toil was done,
They danced and sang and had some fun.

Corrected

Little Shoemakers

Once there were some little **elves**.
They made shoes for shoe store **shelves**.
Their **lives** were filled with pitter-patter.
Making shoes was all that mattered.

Everyone helped—even **wives** and **babies**,
Making shoes for lords and **ladies**.
And when their day's toil was done,
They danced and sang and had some fun.

ANSWER KEYS

Pre-test:
1. B) correct
2. A) loaves
3. A) berries
4. B) correct
5. A) Families

Practice:
1. B) calves
2. B) libraries
3. A) peaches
4. B) knives
5. A) turkeys
6. B) wives
7. B) puppies
8. B) leaves
9. A) valleys
10. B) daisies

Post-test:
1. A) thieves
2. B) correct
3. A) loaves
4. B) correct
5. A) groceries

**Practice With a Purpose—
Plurals—Making Changes**

1. calves
2. wolves
3. babies
4. Families
5. puppies

Name_____ Date_____

Spelling Plurals—Making Changes

Read the poem. Use the rules you have learned about forming plurals of words ending in *-f* or *-fe* and those ending in a single consonant plus *-y* to find and circle the misspelled words. Then copy the poem spelled correctly on the lines below.

Little Shoemakers

Once there were some little elfs.
They made shoes for the shoe store shelfs.
Their lifes were filled with pitter-patter.
Making shoes was all that mattered.

Everyone helped—even wifes and babys,
Making shoes for lords and ladys.
And when their day's toil was done,
They danced and sang and had some fun.

_____

_____

_____

_____

_____

_____

_____

_____

_____

_____

Spelling Plurals—Making Changes

Directions: Decide which spelling of the riddle's answer is correct. Write *A* or *B* on the line.

Who Are We?

_____ 1. We are baby cows.
   A) calfs   B) calves

_____ 2. We are places to check out books.
   A) librarys   B) libraries

_____ 3. We are sweet, delicious fruits.
   A) peaches   B) peachies

_____ 4. We are used to cut and slice.
   A) knifes   B) knives

_____ 5. We are famous for our "gobble."
   A) turkeys   B) turkies

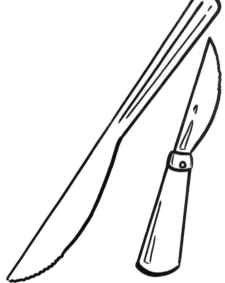

_____ 6. We are our husbands' mates.
   A) wifes   B) wives

_____ 7. We are a dog's babies.
   A) puppys   B) puppies

_____ 8. We are found on trees.
   A) leafs   B) leaves

_____ 9. We are found between mountains.
   A) valleys   B) vallies

_____ 10. We are a bunch of flowers.
   A) daisys   B) daisies

Spelling Plurals—Making Changes

Directions: Decide if the **boldfaced** word is spelled correctly or needs to be changed. Write *A* or *B* on the line next to the matching number.

Cooking is one of my **hobbies**. I love to
(1)
make **loafs** of bread and bake pies filled
(2)
with **berrys** for holiday **parties**. **Familys**
(3)   (4)   (5)
love to feast on my homemade treats.

_____ 1. A) change to hobbys   B) correct
_____ 2. A) change to loaves   B) correct
_____ 3. A) change to berries   B) correct
_____ 4. A) change to partys   B) correct
_____ 5. A) change to Families   B) correct

Spelling Plurals—Making Changes

Directions: Decide if the **boldfaced** word is spelled correctly or needs to be changed. Write *A* or *B* on the line next to the matching number.

(1) Two **thiefs** entered the houses.
(2) The **families** were all in bed.

(3) They sneaked into the kitchen
    to take two **loafs** of bread.

(4) But all the **shelves** were empty, so
(5) they *bought* **grocerys** instead!

_____ 1. A) change to thieves   B) correct
_____ 2. A) change to familys   B) correct
_____ 3. A) change to loaves   B) correct
_____ 4. A) change to shelfs   B) correct
_____ 5. A) change to groceries   B) correct

Related materials for teaching Spelling: Possessives— *'s and s'*
Reproducible: Pre-test and Post-test (page 54); Practice Page (page 53)
Enrichment Activity (page 52)
Rule Book Template (page 6); Individual Record Sheet (page 95)
"Practice With a Purpose": Possessives— *'s and s'* (pages 87-88)

Spelling: Possessives— *'s* and *s'*

The ideas on these three pages follow the flow chart of suggested steps
for teaching, reteaching, and testing presented on page 3 of this book.

STEP 1:
Motivation—Where It Belongs

A common spelling error is to misplace an apostrophe—especially with the letter -s. Much confusion can be cleared up by first pointing out that apostrophes are not used to form plurals. Write these sentences on the board:

The girl went skating.

The girls went skating.

Ask students to explain the difference between the two sentences. (The first is singular—one girl; the second plural—several girls.)

Tell students that you will now write two more sentences, first one about a girl, then one about several girls. Write these sentences:

The girl's skates were new.

The girls' skates were new.

Ask students how this pair of sentences differs from the first pair. (Apostrophes are used.) Ask what the apostrophes represent in these sentences. (Ownership)

Review the meanings of the words *plural* (more than one) and *possessive* (showing ownership). Tell students that one use for apostrophes is to show ownership, but that apostrophes are *not* used to form plurals! (See also plurals lessons on pages 37-42 and 43-48.)

Next, write several pairs of sentences, with one sentence in each pair containing a possessive. Challenge students to find the sentences containing possessives—words showing ownership.* Here are some suggested sentence pairs:

- My **friends** arrived early.
  I held my **friend's** ticket.
- The **teachers** assigned us to groups.
  The **teachers'** groups boarded the bus.
- Four **groups** attended the concert.
  Each **group's** leader signed in.
- **Charles** does not drive.
  Charles's sister picked us up.

The second sentence in each pair contains the possessive.

STEP 2:
Pre-test and Grouping for Instruction

The focus of this lesson is on spelling possessives—singular and plural. If your students still need practice differentiating possessives from plurals, review plurals (pages 37-42 and 43-48) before testing students on possessives. When you feel students are ready for possessives, give them the written pre-test (page 54). Record (or have students record) their scores on an individual record sheet (page 95). Sort through the record sheets and remove the tests of students who scored 100%. You may choose to give these students the post-test right away to verify mastery or wait to give it to them with the rest of the class. Form a group of students who scored 80% or lower for direct instruction and practice.

STEP 3:
Instruction

Present students with the same sentences used in the motivational activity or other sentences containing simple plurals, singular possessives, and plural possessives. (If you are using "Practice With a Purpose" coordinated mini-charts, use the rule page with this lesson.)

Begin by presenting the sentences one at a time for analysis. Filling in the following chart may help clarify the use of *s, 's,* and *s'.* Before introducing the rules for spelling possessives, point out that words ending in *-s* that are not meant to show ownership do NOT contain apostrophes.

	Singular or Plural?	Shows Ownership?	USE
• My **friends** arrived early.	plural	no	no apostrophe
• I held my **friend's** ticket.	**singular**	**yes**	**'s**
• The **teachers** assigned us to groups.	plural	no	no apostrophe
• The **teachers'** groups boarded the bus.	**plural**	**yes**	**s'**
• Four **groups** attended the concert.	plural	no	no apostrophe
• Each **group's** leader signed in.	**singular**	**yes**	**'s**
• **Charles** does not drive.	singular	no	no apostrophe
• **Charles's** sister picked us up.	**singular**	**yes**	**'s ***

** NOTE: It is also correct to use **s'** in a singular possessive that already ends in **-s** (Charle**s'**), for convenience of pronunciation.*

RULE 1 **Use 's to show ownership by a single person, place, thing, or group.**

Example: What are your **team's** colors?

RULE 2 **Use s' to show ownership by more than one person, place, thing, or group.**

Example: Both **teams'** coaches are good.

OPTION: If the owner's name already ends in *-s*, you may just add an '.
Examples: **Wes'** coat was warm. I borrowed **Chris'** bike.

STEP 4:
Apply and Practice

Following direct instruction, give students the opportunity to apply the skill in practice. You may use the prepared practice sheet provided (page 53), side two of the "Practice With a Purpose" mini-chart (page 88), or your own practice sentences. Students can use plain writing paper to copy and correct sentences you write on the board or those provided on the mini-chart. If you choose to use the reproducible practice sheet, duplicate only the number needed for your instructional group. (Use the pre-test results to determine the exact number of students who will need practice.)

Practice may be guided or done independently. Students may work individually, in pairs, or as a group. Correct the page together or privately to assess the need for reteaching before giving the post-test.

STEP 5:
Post-test and Reteaching

When your students have had sufficient instruction and practice, give the post-test. After recording scores on the individual record sheets, once again separate the sheets of those students who scored 80% or less on the post-test for reteaching. You may use or reuse any of the materials suggested in Step 4 for reteaching.

Follow-up / Enrichment

Once students have mastered the skill, make certain they retain it by giving a follow-up activity several weeks later. An excellent way to do this is to see if they can apply the skill in context. Below is a humorous poem you can copy onto chart paper to check for retention. Or, if you prefer, use the prepared reproducible activity sheet on the following page. Have students find and correct any spelling errors. **Tip!** Invite students to write a poem in the same rhyming pattern.

To be corrected

Best Dressed

Long ago stood a castle rare.
Two princesses once lived there.
These spoiled kings daughters
Both begged of their father
To buy them grand dresses to wear.

The tailors great talents were known
By the kingdoms fine tapestries shown.
So he stitched up and down,
But the princesses gowns
Looked just like the rugs that he'd sewn.

Corrected

Best Dressed

Long ago stood a castle rare.
Two princesses once lived there.
These spoiled **king's** daughters
Both begged of their father
To buy them grand dresses to wear.

The **tailor's** great talents were known
By the **kingdom's** fine tapestries shown.
So he stitched up and down,
But the **princesses'** gowns
Looked just like the rugs that he'd sewn.

ANSWER KEYS

Pre-test:

1. A) correct
2. B) Giants'
3. B) Tom's
4. A) correct
5. A) correct

Practice:

1. A) correct
2. B) instruments'
3. A) correct
4. B) Earth's
5. A) correct

6. B) council's
7. B) humans'
8. B) Sherlos'
9. A) correct
10. B) Earthlings'

Post-test:

1. A) correct
2. B) horses'
3. B) ringmaster's
4. A) correct
5. B) performers'

**Practice With a Purpose—
Possessives—*'s* and *s'***

1. author's
2. children's; world's
3. Theodor's

4. Grinch's
5. books'; master's

Spelling Possessives

Read the poem. Use the rules you have learned about possessives to spot the misspelled words. Then copy the poem correctly on the lines below.

Best Dressed

Long ago stood a castle rare.
Two princesses once lived there.
These spoiled kings daughters
Both begged of their father
To buy them grand dresses to wear.

The tailors great talents were known
By the kingdoms fine tapestries shown.
So he stitched up and down,
But the princesses gowns
Looked just like the rugs that he'd sewn.

_____

_____

_____

_____

_____

_____

_____

_____

_____

_____

Possessives—'s and s'

Directions: Imagine that you are the news editor. Write *A* if the possessive (underlined) is correct and *B* if it is incorrect.

ANS (Alien News Service), Planet Sangolius
Dateline—January 30, 2075

_____ 1. Our <u>planet's</u> scientists have spotted a UFO approaching Sangolius.

_____ 2. Their <u>instrument's</u> readings indicate that it may be from Earth.

_____ 3. We have monitored other <u>planets'</u> activities for years.

_____ 4. Until now, it was believed that <u>Earths'</u> satellites were not capable of traveling this far.

_____ 5. Earthlings are said to be a friendly people and would respect <u>Sangolius's</u> land and laws during their visit.

_____ 6. Despite the high <u>councils'</u> advice to remain calm, some Sangolian people remain nervous.

_____ 7. Sherlos, a Sangolian we interviewed, said he had heard that all <u>human's</u> eyes were on their head!

_____ 8. Even if <u>Sherlo's</u> information is right, other Sangolians feel humans are not to be feared simply because they look so different.

_____ 9. Perhaps Earthlings will think the <u>Sangolians'</u> looks are strange!

_____ 10. A neighbor summed it up this way, "Even if the <u>Earthlings</u> hair grows right out of their heads, they have come all this way to meet us. Let's welcome them."

BONUS! Rewrite the news correctly.

Name _____ **Date** _____ **Score** _____

Possessives—'s and s'

Directions: If the sentence is correct as is, write *A* on the line. If it contains an error in the possessive, write *B* on the line.

_____ 1. Chris's big brother, Tom, plays football for the Giants.

_____ 2. Chris goes to all the Giant's home games.

_____ 3. Last night Toms' tackle saved a touchdown.

_____ 4. The crowd's cheers made Chris feel proud.

_____ 5. Someday Chris hopes to follow in his brother's footsteps and play for the Giants.

Name _____ **Date** _____ **Score** _____

Possessives—'s and s'

Directions: If the sentence is correct as is, write *A* on the line. If it contains an error in the possessive, write *B* on the line.

_____ 1. For Alexis' birthday, her aunt took her to the circus.

_____ 2. Alexis gasped when the riders stood on the horse's backs.

_____ 3. She cheered when the ringmasters' voice counted aloud as 20 clowns came out of one car.

_____ 4. When the tightrope walker's foot slipped, Alexis hid her face for a moment in her aunt's shoulder, then laughed when she didn't fall.

_____ 5. Alexis enjoyed all the performer's circus acts.

Related materials for teaching Spelling: Help With *ie* and *ei*
Reproducible: Pre-test and Post-test (page 60); Practice Page (page 59)
Enrichment Activity (page 58)
Rule Book Template (page 6); Individual Record Sheet (page 95)
"Practice With a Purpose": Help With *ie* and *ei* (pages 89-90)

Spelling: Help With *ie* and *ei*

The ideas on these three pages follow the flow chart of suggested steps for teaching, reteaching, and testing presented on page 3 of this book.

STEP 1:
In Brief

The spelling of words such as *believe, receive, neighbor,* and *neither* can be particularly troublesome because of the seemingly arbitrary use of *ie* and *ei.* Even adults with good spelling skills may find themselves muttering the "*i* before *e . . .*" chant under their breath as they write a word such as *receipt.* Although that rule is useful and is presented below, there are exceptions. Begin helping students sort out this tricky spelling problem by presenting several sentences that include words in which the *ie* or *ei* is missing. Ask students to supply the correct missing letters. Here are some suggestions.

- There is a fly on the **c__ling**.
- Did you **rec__ve** my card?
- It was **th__r** first trip.
- I cannot **bel__ve** it is here already.
- The cool breeze was a **rel__f**.

- Mr. Jones is my **n__ghbor**.
- The jewels were stolen by a **th__f**.
- I made a new **fr__nd** at camp.
- The package **w__ghed** two pounds.
- The speech was **br__f** and to the point.

STEP 2:
Pre-test and Grouping for Instruction

Check students' ability to recognize the correct spelling of representative words containing *ie* or *ei* by giving all students the written pre-test (page 60). Record (or have students record) their scores on an individual record sheet (page 95). Sort through the record sheets and remove the tests of students who scored 100%. You may choose to give these students the post-test right away to verify mastery or wait to give it to them with the rest of the class. Form a group of students who scored 80% or lower for direct instruction and practice.

STEP 3:
Instruction

Present students with the sentences used in the motivational activity. Fill in the correct letter combinations for students to observe. Explain that although this rule is helpful, there are a number of words that do not follow the rule. Since the word *weird* is one common exception, suggest to students that they remember the listed exceptions as "weird" words. Present the following general rule. (If you are using the "Practice With a Purpose" coordinated mini-charts, use the rule page with this lesson.)

RULE 1 👉 **Generally, use *i* before *e*, except after *c*, or when the vowel pair sounds like *a*, as in *weigh*.**

"Weird" exceptions—
weird, either, neither, seize, leisure, their

Prepare a chart like the one below. Begin with the key words used in the motivational sentences. Challenge students to place each of those words in the correct section; then add more words to the chart.

There is a fly on the **ceiling**.   Mr. Jones is my **neighbor**.
Did you **receive** my card?   The jewels were stolen by a **thief**.
It was **their** first trip.   I made a new **friend** at camp.
I cannot **believe** it is here already.   The package **weighed** two pounds.
The cool breeze was a **relief**.   The speech was **brief** and to the point.

i before *e*	*e* before *i* (follows a *c*)	*e* before *i* (sounds like *a*)	"weird" exceptions
believe	ceiling	neighbor	weird
relief	receive	weighed	either
thief	receipt	sleigh	neither
friend	perceive	eight	leisure
brief			their
fierce			

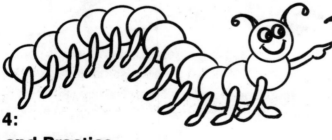

See if students notice the pattern in the third column—the ei sounds like a and is followed by gh.

STEP 4:
Apply and Practice

Following direct instruction, give students the opportunity to apply the skill in practice. You may use the prepared practice sheet provided (page 59), side two of of the "Practice With a Purpose" mini-chart (page 90), or your own practice sentences. Students can use plain writing paper to copy and correct sentences you write on the board or those provided on the mini-chart. If you choose to use the reproducible practice sheet, duplicate only the number needed for your instructional group. (Use the pre-test results to determine the exact number of students who will need practice.)

Practice may be guided or done independently. Students may work individually, in pairs, or as a group. Correct the page together or privately to assess the need for reteaching before giving the post-test.

STEP 5:
Post-test and Reteaching

When your students have had sufficient instruction and practice, give the post-test. After recording scores on the individual record sheets, once again separate the sheets of those students who scored 80% or less on the post-test for reteaching. You may use or reuse any of the materials suggested in Step 4 for reteaching.

Follow-up / Enrichment

Once students have mastered the skill, make certain they retain it by giving a follow-up activity several weeks later. An excellent way to do this is to see if they can apply the skill in context. Below is a story you can copy onto chart paper to check for retention. Have students rewrite the story correctly. Or, if you prefer, use the prepared reproducible activity sheet on the following page. **Tip!** Invite students to write their own stories about a real or imagined amusement park.

To be corrected

Leisure Land

The other night I had a wierd dream. My nice, quiet nieghborhood had turned into an amusement park. At first I could not beleive it; then a freind appeared at my door with free tickets to all the rides.

We rode giant roller coasters and ate cotton candy until niether of us could take another bite. I was releived to wake up in my own bed—ready for a day that was completely right-side up and meals that were not pink! Perhaps it is better for my stomach that my visit to Liesure Land was just a dream!

Corrected

Leisure Land

The other night I had a **weird** dream. My nice, quiet **neighborhood** had turned into an amusement park. At first I could not **believe** it; then a **friend** appeared at my door with free tickets to all the rides.

We rode giant roller coasters and ate cotton candy until **neither** of us could take another bite. I was **relieved** to wake up in my own bed—ready for a day that was completely right-side up and meals that were not pink! Perhaps it is better for my stomach that my visit to **Leisure** Land was just a dream!

 ANSWER KEYS

Pre-test:

1. B) ~~queit~~ quiet
2. A) correct
3. A) correct
4. B) ~~siezed~~ seized
5. A) correct

Practice:

1. A) neighborhood
2. B) quiet
3. B) friend
4. A) weird
5. B) Neither
6. B) ceiling
7. A) seize
8. B) thief
9. A) mischief
10. B) relief

Post-test:

1. A) correct
2. A) correct
3. A) correct
4. B) ~~recieves~~ receives
5. B) ~~releif~~ relief

**Practice With a Purpose—
Help With *ie* and *ei***

1. ~~freind~~ friend; briefly *correct as is*
2. piece *correct as is*
3. weird *correct as is*
4. Believing *correct as is;* ~~nieghbor's~~ neighbor's
5. thief *correct as is*

Spelling Words With *ie* and *ei*

Read the story. Use the rules you have learned about spelling words containing *ie* and *ei* to find the misspelled words. Then copy the story correctly on the lines below.

Leisure Land

The other night I had a wierd dream.
My nice, quiet nieghborhood had turned into an
amusement park. At first I could not beleive it; then
a freind appeared at my door with free tickets to all the rides.

We rode giant roller coasters and ate cotton candy until niether
of us could take another bite. I was releived to wake up in my own bed—
ready for a day that was completely right-side up and meals that were not pink!
Perhaps it is better for my stomach that my visit to Liesure Land was just a dream!

_____

_____

_____

_____

_____

_____

_____

_____

_____

_____

_____

_____

_____

_____

Help With *ie* and *ei*

Directions: Write the letter of the answer that is spelled correctly.

The Attic

1. A) neighborhood B) nieghborhood

2. A) queit B) quiet

3. A) freind B) friend

4. A) weird B) wierd

5. A) Niether B) Neither

6. A) cieling B) ceiling

7. A) seize B) sieze

8. A) theif B) thief

9. A) mischief B) mischeif

10. A) releif B) relief

Our _____ is usually _____.
(1)   (2)
But one night, just after dark, my

_____ and I heard a _____ sound.
(3)   (4)
_____ of us could quite describe it,
(5)
but it sounded like it was coming

from the _____! Flashlight in hand,
(6)
we climbed the attic stairs, prepared

to _____ a _____. But what did we
(7)   (8)
find making all that _____? Just
(9)
a family of owls. What a _____!
(10)

Pre-test

Name _____ **Date** _____ **Score** _____

Help With *ie* and *ei*

Directions: Find the word containing *ie* or *ei* in each sentence. Write *A* if the sentence is correct as is, or *B* if a spelling change is needed.

_____ 1. It was so queit that I didn't notice it at first.
   A) correct   B) change *queit* to *quiet*

_____ 2. Without a sound, it creeped along the ceiling.
   A) correct   B) change *ceiling* to *cieling*

_____ 3. Then, like a thief, it struck without warning.
   A) correct   B) change *thief* to *theif*

_____ 4. It siezed the fly before it could land on my lunch.
   A) correct   B) change *siezed* to *seized*

_____ 5. Some would disagree, but a spider can be your friend.
   A) correct   B) change *friend* to *freind*

Post-test

Name _____ **Date** _____ **Score** _____

Help With *ie* and *ei*

Directions: Find the word containing *ie* or *ei* in each sentence. Write *A* if the sentence is correct as is, or *B* if a spelling change is needed.

_____ 1. Do you believe that a teacher gives grades?
   A) correct   B) change *believe* to *beleive*

_____ 2. This may sound weird, but I don't believe it.
   A) correct   B) change *weird* to *wierd*

_____ 3. I think a person either works hard or doesn't.
   A) correct   B) change *either* to *iether*

_____ 4. A person earns whatever grade he or she recieves.
   A) correct   B) change *recieves* to *receives*

_____ 5. The teacher just records it—now isn't that a releif?
   A) correct   B) change *releif* to *relief*

Tom P.   A
English
1. Advantage
2. Percentac
3. Mortgage
4. Adage
5. Cabbage

Related materials for teaching Spelling: *Then / Than; Of / Have*
Reproducible: Pre-test and Post-test (page 66); Practice Page (page 65)
Enrichment Activity (page 64)
Rule Book Template (page 6); Individual Record Sheet (page 95)
"Practice With a Purpose": Not the Same—*Then / Than; Of / Have* (pages 91-92)

Spelling: *Then / Than; Of / Have*

The ideas on these three pages follow the flow chart of suggested steps for teaching, reteaching, and testing presented on page 3 of this book.

STEP 1:

Motivation—
I Could Of Done Better Then That!

Spelling errors sometimes involve mix-ups of words. Two common cases are the substitution of *then* for *than* and *of* for *have*. Ask students if they have ever heard someone say, "I'm faster then you." or "I could of gone." Next, say or write several sentences with *then* used for *than* and *of* used for *have* in some cases. Ask students to find the errors. Here are some suggested sentences:

(then for than)

- My brother is older **then** yours.
- We ate and **then** we went on a hike. *(correct)*
- This bug is tinier **then** the others.
- It's farther **then** that!

(of for have)

- I should **of** been on time.
- She couldn't **of** seen it.
- Dale would **of** given me a ride.
- We shouldn't **have** eaten so much! *(correct)*

STEP 2:
Pre-test and Grouping for Instruction

Even if your students recognize the misuse of *then / than* and *of / have* in the oral exercises, make certain they can differentiate the two terms in writing by giving all students the written pre-test (page 66). Record (or have students record) their scores on an individual record sheet (page 95). Sort through the record sheets and remove the tests of students who scored 100%. You may choose to give these students the post-test right away to verify mastery or wait to give it to them with the rest of the class. Form a group of students who scored 80% or lower for direct instruction and practice.

STEP 3:
Instruction

Present students with the same sentences used in the motivational activity or other examples with the same types of substitutions. Present one general rule for differentiating between *then* and *than* and another one for differentiating *of* from *have*. (If you are using "Practice With a Purpose" coordinated mini-charts, use the rule page for this lesson.) Guide students to discover these rules:

RULE 1 *Then* means *when*.

Than is used *to compare*.

Have students test each sentence by asking if it tells *when* or *compares* items:

✗ My brother is older **then** yours.
   (Compares, so use *than*.)
   My brother is older **than** yours.

✓ We ate and **then** we went on a hike.
   (Tells when, so use *then*. Correct.)

✗ This bug is tinier **then** the others.
   (Compares, so use *than*.)
   This bug is tinier **than** the others.

✗ It's further **then** that!
   (Compares, so use *than*.)
   It's farther **than** that!

RULE 2 You always *HAVE*, but you never must *of*, could *of*, would *of*, or should *of*!

In these cases when you say *of* it sounds like *ov*, which is really -'*ve*, which means *have*. Check the meaning against the spelling used:

✗ I **should of** been on time. (Means *should've*, which is short for *should have*.)
   I **should've** been on time.

✗ She **couldn't of** seen it. (Means *couldn't have*, which is short for *could not have*.)
   She **couldn't have** seen it.

✗ Dale **would of** given me a ride. (Means *would've*, which is short for *would have*.)

✓ We **shouldn't have** eaten so much. (Means *should not have*. Correct.)

STEP 4:
Apply and Practice

Following direct instruction, give students the opportunity to apply the skill in practice. You may use the prepared practice sheet provided (page 65), side two of the "Practice With a Purpose" mini-chart (page 92), or your own practice sentences. Students can use plain writing paper to copy and correct sentences you write on the board or those provided on the mini-chart. If you choose to use the reproducible practice sheet, duplicate only the number needed for your instructional group. (Use the pre-test results to determine the exact number of students who will need practice.)

Practice may be guided or done independently. Students may work individually, in pairs, or as a group. Correct the page together or privately to assess the need for reteaching before giving the post-test.

STEP 5:
Post-test and Reteaching

When your students have had sufficient instruction and practice, give the post-test. After recording scores on the individual record sheets, once again separate the sheets of those students who scored 80% or less on the post-test for reteaching. You may use or reuse any of the materials suggested in Step 4 for reteaching.

Follow-up / Enrichment

Once students have mastered the skill, make certain they retain it by giving a follow-up activity several weeks later. An excellent way to do this is to see if they can apply the skill in context. Below is a humorous poem you can copy onto chart paper to check for retention. Or, if you prefer, use the prepared reproducible activity sheet on the following page. Have students find and correct the errors. **Tip!** Invite students to write their own poems about visitors from other worlds.

To be corrected

People Sighting
I thought the story was a fake.
It couldn't of been true.
It made me do a double take,
But then I saw him, too!

His ship was bigger then a bus,
And *he* must of weighed a ton!
But you should of seen him look at *us*,
Than turn his back and run!

Corrected

People Sighting
I thought the story was a fake.
It **couldn't have** been true.
It made me do a double take,
But <u>then</u> I saw him, too!

His ship was bigger **than** a bus,
And *he* **must have** weighed a ton!
But you **should have** seen him look at *us*,
Then turn his back and run!

ANSWER KEYS

Pre-test:
1. A) then
2. B) than
3. B) have
4. B) have
5. B) than

Practice:
1. B) have
2. B) have
3. A) of
4. B) than
5. B) have

6. A) Then
7. B) have
8. B) have
9. B) than
10. B) than

Post-test:
1. A) then
2. B) than
3. B) have
4. B) than
5. B) have

Practice With a Purpose—
Not the Same–
Then/Than; Of/Have

1. I could **have** been . . . I might **have** . . .
2. I could have been . . . I could **have** . . .
3. I could have been . . . **Than** anyone . . .

4. I could have signed . . .
    Than anyone . . .
5. could have . . .

Not the Same—*Then / Than; Of / Have*

Read the poem. Use the rules you have learned about mistaking *then* for *than* and *of* for *have* to find the spelling errors. Then copy the poem correctly on the lines below.

People Sighting

I thought the story was a fake.
It couldn't of been true.
It made me do a double take,
But then I saw him, too!

His ship was bigger then a bus,
And *he* must of weighed a ton!
But you should of seen him look at *us*,
Than turn his back and run!

_____

_____

_____

_____

_____

_____

_____

_____

_____

_____

_____

Spelling *Then* / *Than* and *Of* / *Have*

Directions: On the line before each sentence, write the letter of the word that belongs in the blank.

To Be a Dinosaur

_____ 1. It must _____ been grand to be a dinosaur.
A) of   B) have

_____ 2. If I could _____ been one, I would have been a Tyrannosaurus.
A) of   B) have

_____ 3. Everyone would have gotten out _____ my way.
A) of   B) have

_____ 4. My teeth would have been bigger _____ anyone else's.
A) then   B) than

_____ 5. I would _____ tromped around making thunder with my feet.
A) of   B) have

_____ 6. _____ I would have stopped and found some other dinosaur to eat.
A) Then   B) Than

_____ 7. The dinosuars would all _____ been afraid of me.
A) of   B) have

_____ 8. There is nothing I couldn't _____ done!
A) of   B) have

_____ 9. I would have been bigger and stronger _____ any other living thing!
A) then   B) than

_____ 10. BUT I think I would rather be me _____ a dinosaur, because dinosaurs *are* no more!
A) then   B) than

Name _____ **Date** _____ **Score** _____

Spelling *Then / Than* and *Of / Have*

Directions: On the line before each sentence, write the letter of the word that belongs in the blank.

_____ 1. I ate dinner and _____ did my homework.
    A) then   B) than

_____ 2. The assignment was harder _____ I expected.
    A) then   B) than

_____ 3. I should _____ paid more attention in class!
    A) of   B) have

_____ 4. I must ___ missed what the teacher said about atoms.
    A) of   B) have

_____ 5. Are they bigger or smaller _____ molecules?
    A) then   B) than

Name _____ **Date** _____ **Score** _____

Spelling *Then / Than* and *Of / Have*

Directions: On the line before each sentence, write the letter of the word that belongs in the blank.

_____ 1. Our team warmed up and _____ went out on the field.
    A) then   B) than

_____ 2. The other players seemed bigger _____ ours.
    A) then   B) than

_____ 3. They must _____ thought we would be easy to beat.
    A) of   B) have

_____ 4. But, it turned out that we were stronger _____ they were.
    A) then   B) than

_____ 5. We only won by three points, but it should _____ been more!
    A) of   B) have

             FS-10171 Plain English—Spelling

Related materials for teaching Spelling: Prickly Pairs
Reproducible: Pre-test and Post-test (page 72); Practice Page (page 71)
Enrichment Activity (page 70)
Rule Book Template (page 6); Individual Record Sheet (page 95)
"Practice With a Purpose": Prickly Pairs (pages 93-94)

Spelling: Prickly Pairs

The ideas on these three pages follow the flow chart of suggested steps for teaching, reteaching, and testing presented on page 3 of this book.

STEP 1:
Motivation—Slightly Different

This lesson covers eight pairs of words that sound similar and are often interchanged. Present each pair. Have students compare spellings. Challenge them to define each word and use it in a sentence.

- **capital**
  capitol
- **accept**
  except
- **loose**
  lose
- **medal**
  metal
- **desert**
  dessert
- **already**
  all ready
- **past**
  passed
- **stationary**
  stationery

STEP 2:
Pre-test and Grouping for Instruction

Follow the introduction by giving all students the written pre-test (page 72). Record (or have students record) their scores on an individual record sheet (page 95). Sort through the record sheets and remove the tests of students who scored 100%. You may choose to give these students the post-test right away to verify mastery or wait to give it to them with the rest of the class. Form a group of students who scored 80% or lower for direct instruction and practice.

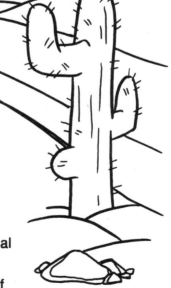

STEP 3:
Instruction

Present students with the word pairs and simple definitions, such as those below. (If you are using the "Practice With a Purpose" coordinated mini-charts, use the rule page for this lesson.)

- ✓ **capital** = a city
- ✓ **accept** = receive
- ✓ **loose** = not tight
- ✓ **medal** = an award
- ✓ **desert** = a dry region
- ✓ **already** = previously
- ✓ **past** = over, already happened
- ✓ **stationary** = in a fixed position

- ✓ **capitol** = a building
- ✓ **except** = leave out
- ✓ **lose** = misplace, not win
- ✓ **metal** = a mineral
- ✓ **dessert** = treat after a meal
- ✓ **all ready** = all are ready
- ✓ **passed** = moved ahead of
- ✓ **stationery** = writing paper

RULE 1 Check the spelling against the intended meaning.

Explain to students that the English language is filled with similar-sounding words. Misuse of these may go unnoticed in speaking but is glaringly evident in writing. Even computer word processing programs that provide spell-checkers cannot be relied upon to spot these errors. Write this sentence on the board to illustrate why "prickly pairs" are so troublesome: *I all ready used the spell-checker and I except the computer's judgment.*

The program is designed to recognize misspelled words, and, in fact, there are none in the sentence. But, in the context of intended meaning, there are two errors: *all ready* should be spelled *already*, and *except* should be *accept.* Remind students that writing is produced for people, not computers, and it is ultimately people who must decipher intended meaning. That is why this rule is so important, not only with regard to the eight prickly pairs highlighted here, but in all writing.

Extend this lesson to include other "prickly pairs"—words that are often interchanged. Beginning with the eight pairs listed on page 67, make a Prickly Pair reference chart to keep on display. Write each word and a simple definition. Then challenge students to add more troublesome pairs as they encounter them. The box on the right offers additional common ones.

affect = influence
effect = bring about

all ways = in every way
always = at all times

complement = a completing part
compliment = flattering remark

imply = to hint at
infer = draw a conclusion

lay = to place
lie = to recline

*Lay the pillow in Spotty's bed.
He wants to lie down.*

STEP 4:
Apply and Practice

Following direct instruction, give students the opportunity to apply the skill in practice. You may use the prepared practice sheet provided (page 71), side two of the "Practice With a Purpose" mini-chart (page 94), or your own practice sentences. Students can use plain writing paper to copy and correct sentences you write on the board or those provided on the mini-chart. If you choose to use the reproducible practice sheet, duplicate only the number needed for your instructional group. (Use the pre-test results to determine the exact number of students who will need practice.)

Practice may be guided or done independently. Students may work individually, in pairs, or as a group. Correct the page together or privately to assess the need for reteaching before giving the post-test.

STEP 5:
Post-test and Reteaching

When your students have had sufficient instruction and practice, give the post-test. After recording scores on the individual record sheets, once again separate the sheets of those students who scored 80% or less on the post-test for reteaching. You may use or reuse any of the materials suggested in Step 4 for reteaching.

Follow-up / Enrichment

Once students have mastered the skill, make certain they retain it by giving a follow-up activity several weeks later. An excellent way to do this is to see if they can apply the skill in context. Have students rewrite the story choosing the correct spelling from each word pair. Or, if you prefer, use the prepared reproducible activity page that follows. **Tip!** Let students finish the story with their own ideas about what the archeologists found.

To be corrected

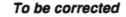

In Search of the <u>Past/Passed</u>

The archeologists gathered in Cairo, the <u>capital/capitol</u> of Egypt, to prepare for the journey into the <u>desert/dessert.</u> They had <u>already/all ready</u> been instructed to pack <u>loose/lose</u> clothing and take nothing <u>accept/except</u> essentials. Once they arrived at the site, they would set up a <u>stationary/stationery</u> camp. Then, for the next three months, they would spend their days digging for secrets of the <u>past/passed</u>.

Corrected

In Search of the <u>Past</u>

The archeologists gathered in Cairo, the **capital** of Egypt, to prepare for the journey into the **desert**. They had **already** been instructed to pack **loose** clothing and take nothing **except** essentials. Once they arrived at the site, they would set up a **stationary** camp. Then, for the next three months, they would spend their days digging for secrets of the **past**.

ANSWER KEYS

Pre-test:

1. B) ~~accept~~ except
2. C) ~~medal~~ metal
3. A) correct
4. B) ~~past~~ passed
5. A) correct

Practice:

ACROSS:
2. B) passed
5. A) accept
7. A) loose
8. A) desert
9. B) lose

DOWN:
1. A) capital
3. B) stationery
4. B) except
5. A) already
6. B) metal

Post-test:

1. B) ~~stationary~~ stationery
2. B) ~~metal~~ medal
3. A) ~~accept~~ except
4. A) ~~loose~~ lose
5. B) ~~except~~ accept

**Practice With a Purpose—
Prickly Pairs**

1. lose; time
2. capital; Paris
3. dessert; ice cream
4. metal; gold
5. accept; apology

Name_____ Date_____

Spelling Prickly Pairs

Read the story. Choose the word from each pair whose spelling matches the intended meaning. Then copy the story correctly on the lines below.

In Search of the Past/Passed

The archeologists gathered in Cairo, the capital/capitol of Egypt, to prepare for the journey into the desert/dessert. They had already/all ready been instructed to pack loose/lose clothing and take nothing accept/except essentials. Once they arrived at the site, they would set up a stationary/stationery camp. Then, for the next three months, they would spend their days digging for secrets of the past/passed.

_____
_____
_____
_____
_____
_____
_____
_____
_____
_____

Spelling Prickly Pairs

Directions: On each line write the letter of the correct spelling for the clue given. Then write the answer in the puzzle.

ACROSS

_____ 2. moved ahead of
A) past   B) passed

_____ 5. receive
A) accept   B) except

_____ 7. not tight
A) loose   B) lose

_____ 8. a dry region
A) desert   B) dessert

_____ 9. misplace, not win
A) loose   B) lose

DOWN

_____ 1. a city
A) capital   B) capitol

_____ 3. writing paper
A) stationary   B) stationery

_____ 4. leave out
A) accept   B) except

_____ 5. previously
A) already   B) all ready

_____ 6. a mineral
A) medal   B) metal

Name _____ **Date** _____ **Score** _____

Spelling Prickly Pairs

Directions: Think about the intended meaning of each sentence. Write the letter of the change, if any, that is needed.

_____ 1. All accept Dave were on board flight 232 to Phoenix, the capital of Arizona.
A) correct   B) change *accept* to *except*   C) change *capital* to *capitol*

_____ 2. We had already gone through the medal detector and checked in.
A) correct   B) change *already* to *all ready*   C) change *medal* to *metal*

_____ 3. "How could he lose something as important as his plane ticket?" I thought.
A) correct   B) change *lose* to *loose*   C) change *thought* to *though*

_____ 4. After a few minutes had past, Dave finally showed up—ticket in hand.
A) correct   B) change *past* to *passed*   C) change *past* to *pass*

_____ 5. At last, we took off for our trip to the desert!
A) correct   B) change *off* to *of*   C) change *desert* to *dessert*

Name _____ **Date** _____ **Score** _____

Spelling Prickly Pairs

Directions: In each sentence find a word that does not express the intended meaning. Write the letter of the change that would correct it.

_____ 1. Enter and win the "Save Our Desert Wildlife" contest and you could receive a letter from the president on his personal stationary!
A) change *Desert* to *Dessert*   B) change *stationary* to *stationery*

_____ 2. Winners will also go to our capital, Washington, D.C., and receive a metal.
A) change *capital* to *capitol*   B) change *metal* to *medal*

_____ 3. All entries will be considered accept those received after the deadline has passed.   A) change *accept* to *except*   B) change *passed* to *past*

_____ 4. There's no time to loose, so don't delay! Mail your entry today!
A) change *loose* to *lose*   B) change *Mail* to *Male*

_____ 5. Perhaps you will be one of the winners to stand on the steps of the capitol and except a medal for helping to save our desert wildlife!
A) change *capitol* to *capital*   B) change *except* to *accept*

Sound-Alikes *Its* and *It's*

① *Its* Belongs to It

Like *his* and *her*, *its* shows ownership.
Use *its* when you mean <u>belongs to it</u>.

✔ *Its* foot is never on the ground.
(foot belongs to it)

✔ It never turns *its* head.
(head belongs to it)

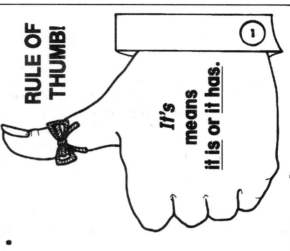

RULE OF THUMB!

Its
means
<u>belongs to it.</u>

RULE OF THUMB!

It's
means
<u>it is or it has.</u>

② *It's* Just for Short

As in *he's* and *she's*, the *'s* in *it's*
is short for <u>is</u> or <u>has</u>. Use *it's* when
you mean <u>it is</u> or <u>it has.</u>

✔ *It's* been waiting here all day for you. (It has)

✔ Now *it's* time to go to bed! (it is)

Practice With a Purpose
Rule and Reference

Sound-Alikes
Its and *It's*

What Is It?

1. Pick it out from the bunch. Its great to put in your lunch. What is it?

2. Watch out for its prickles. If you get stuck, it doesn't tickle! What is it?

3. It's a tool, that as a rule, is often found and used in school. What is it?

4. In a hurry to get there fast? It's wings will do it if its fuel will last. What is it?

5. When its cold and there is snow, build one of these and name it Joe! What is it?

Riddle answers: 1. banana 2. cactus 3. ruler 4. jet 5. snowman

Sound-Alikes
Its and *It's*

Write each riddle and its solution. Correct any errors you find.

 ruler

 cactus

 mittens

 bird

 hammer

 banana

snowman

 pickle

jet

✓ *Its* means <u>belongs to it</u>.
✓ *It's* means <u>it is or it has</u>.

Practice With a Purpose
Follow-up and Practice

Sound-Alikes
Its and *It's*

FS-10171 Plain English—Spelling

Sound-Alikes *Your* and *You're*

① *Your* Belongs to You

Your shows ownership.
Your means <u>belongs to you.</u>

✔ It is *your* idea. (idea belongs to you)
✔ What's *your* name?
    (name belongs to you)
✘ *Your* early. (early belongs to you? NO)

RULE OF THUMB!

Your means
<u>belongs to you.</u>

①

② *You're* Is the Way You Are

The *'re* in *you're* is short for *are*.
You're is short for <u>you are.</u>

✔ *You're* my friend.   (you are my friend)
✔ I know *you're* coming. (you are coming)
✘ I have *you're* phone number.
    (you are a phone number? NO)

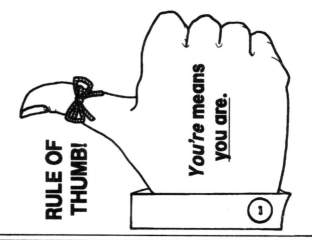

RULE OF THUMB!

You're means
<u>you are.</u>

①

Practice With a Purpose
Rule and Reference

Sound-Alikes
Your and *You're*

Sound-Alikes *Your* and *You're*

Read carefully. Copy each sentence.
Fill in the blank with *your* or *you're*.

Your means
belongs to you.
You're means
you are.

1. Uncle Wes called today.
   ____ to call him back by 6:00.

2. He needs ____ help.

3. He and Aunt Marie are going
   camping near that lake ____
   friend liked so much.

4. He'd like to borrow ____ tent.

5. I told him that ____ free
   Saturday to bring it over and
   show him how to put it up.

Practice With a Purpose
Follow-up and Practice

Sound-Alikes
Your* and *You're

 FS-10171 Plain English—Spelling

Sound-Alikes *Whose* and *Who's*

① Whose Is It?

Whose shows ownership.
Whose means belongs to whom.

✔ *Whose* paper is this?
✔ Name the team *whose* record is best.
✗ I wonder *whose* at the door.
   (does not show ownership)

Whose means belongs to whom.

② Who's There?

As in *it's*, the *'s* in *who's* is short for *is* or
Who's means who is or who has.

✔ *Who's* at the door? (Who is)
✔ *Who's* seen a comet? (Who has)
✔ I'm the one *who's* always late. (who is)
✗ I'm the one *who's* watch stopped.
   (shows ownership; does not mean who is)

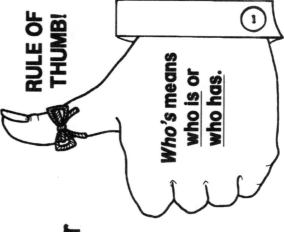

RULE OF
THUMB!

Who's means
who is or
who has.

Practice With a Purpose
Rule and Reference

Sound-Alikes
Whose and *Who's*

Sound-Alikes *Whose* and *Who's*

**Read carefully. Copy each sentence.
Fill in the blank with *whose* or *who's*.**

1. I wonder _____ mailed this package to me.
   _{who has}

2. I don't know anyone _____ from New York.
   _{who is}

3. Perhaps I'm not the one _____ supposed to have received it.
   _{who is}

4. There could be someone else with a name like mine _____ address is also similar.
   _{belongs to whom}

5. I'll have to open the box to see _____ sent it.
   _{who has}

✓ *Whose* means belongs to whom.
✓ *Who's* means who is or who has.

Practice With a Purpose
Follow-up and Practice

Sound-Alikes
Whose* and *Who's

Sound-Alikes
There, Their, and They're

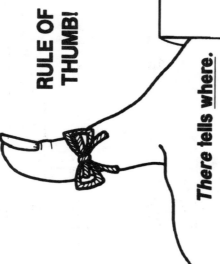

RULE OF THUMB!

There tells where.

Their means belongs to them.

They're means they are.

① **Here and There**

There tells where.

✔ Meet me *there*. (tells where)

② **Their Belongs to Them**

Their shows ownership.
Their means belongs to them.

✔ It's *their* turn. (belongs to them)

③ **They're the Ones**

The *'re* in *they're* is short for are.
They're means they are.

✔ *They're* good sports. (they are)

Practice With a Purpose
Rule and Reference

**Sound-Alikes *There,*
Their, and *They're***

Sound-Alikes
There, Their, and They're

Copy each sentence. Fill in *there*, *their*, or *they're*.

The Costume Party

1. _____ at the door, now!

2. Did you see _____ costumes?

3. I recognize Jeff under _____.

4. Wow! _____ wigs are terrific!

5. Wait _____ a minute while I get the camera!

✔ *There* tells <u>where.</u>   ✔ *Their* means <u>belongs to them.</u>   ✔ *They're* means <u>they are.</u>

Practice With a Purpose
Follow-up and Practice

Sound-Alikes *There, Their,* and *They're*

80   FS-10171 Plain English—Spelling

Sound-Alikes *To*, *Two*, and *Too*

① To Is Part of the Action

To means **move toward** or is part of a **verb** (action).

✔ Come *to* me. (move toward)
✔ We have *to leave*. (verb/action)

② Two Is Number 2

Two is the word for the number 2.

✔ I have *two* feet. (2)

③ Also and Excess, Too

Too can mean **also**. *Too* means **excess**, too (*too* much or *too* little).

✔ It's *too* hot. (excess)
✔ I think it's hot, *too*. (also)

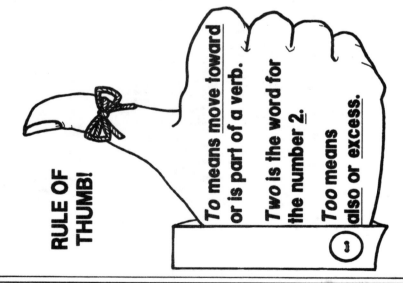

RULE OF THUMB!

To means **move toward** or is part of a verb.

Two is the word for the number **2**.

Too means **also** or **excess**.

Practice With a Purpose
Rule and Reference

Sound-Alikes
To, Two, and *Too*

Sound-Alikes *To*, *Two*, and *Too*

Read carefully. Copy the paragraph.
Correct each misspelling of *to, two,* **or** *too.*

✔ *To* means move toward or is part of a verb.
✔ *Two* is the word for the number 2.
✔ *Too* means also or excess.

(1) Are you going too watch the holiday special on TV tonight? (2) I am, two. (3) Too of my favorite stars are in it. (4) I think some shows have two many commercials, though. (5) Do you think so, to?

Practice With a Purpose
Follow-up and Practice

Sound-Alikes
To, Two, and *Too*

Plurals—Adding -es

Watch for -s, -x, -sh, and -ch.

Plural means <u>more than one.</u> You add -s to most words to make them plural. But watch for words ending in -s, -x, -sh, and -ch. You must add -es to these words.

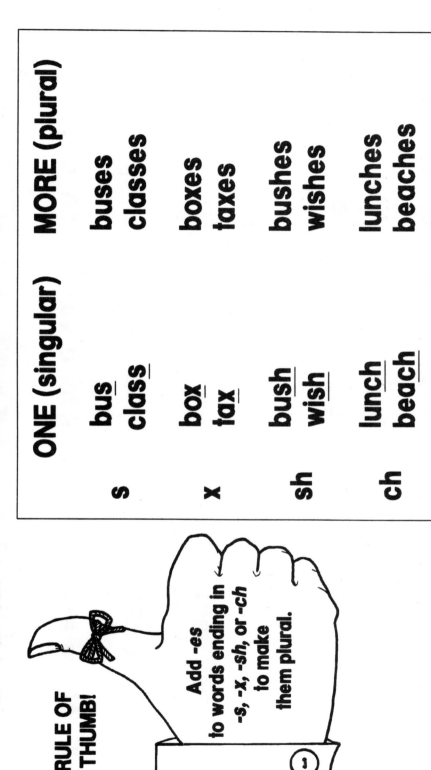

	ONE (singular)	MORE (plural)
s	bus<u> </u>	buses
	class<u> </u>	classes
x	box<u> </u>	boxes
	tax<u> </u>	taxes
sh	bush<u> </u>	bushes
	wish<u> </u>	wishes
ch	lunch<u> </u>	lunches
	beach<u> </u>	beaches

RULE OF THUMB!

Add -es
to words ending in
-s, -x, -sh, or -ch
to make
them plural.

Practice With a Purpose
Rule and Reference

Plurals—
Adding -es

FS-10171 Plain English—Spelling

Plurals—Adding -es

Read carefully. Copy each sentence. Correct each misspelling you find.

1. The children boarded the buses headed for the beachs.

2. They packed their lunches in boxs.

3. The teachers rode with their classes.

4. All were filled with wishs for a warm, bright day.

5. They hoped to need their sunglass's.

✓ Add -es to words ending in -s, -x, -sh, and -ch to make them plural.

Practice With a Purpose
Follow-up and Practice

**Plurals—
Adding -es**

Plurals—Making Changes

① The f ➡ v Switch

To form the plural of most words that end in -f or -fe, change the -f or -fe to -v and add -es.

ONE (singular)	MORE (plural)
half	halves
knife	knives
scarf	scarves

RULE OF THUMB!

Ends in -f or -fe?
Change -f or -fe
to -v and add -es.

② The y ➡ i Switch

...rm the plural of words ending with a ...onant and -y, change the -y to -i and add -es.

ONE (singular)	MORE (plural)
baby	babies
cherry	cherries
family	families
city	cities

RULE OF THUMB!

Ends in a
consonant
plus -y?
Change the -y to -i
and add -es.

Practice With a Purpose
Rule and Reference

**Plurals—
Making Changes**

Plurals—Making Changes

Copy each sentence. Look at the picture clues. Fill in the missing plural. Use the rules to spell it correctly.

✔ To form the plural of words ending with a consonant and -y, change the -y to -i and add -es.

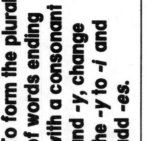
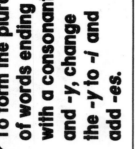

baby cow—
calf

baby wolf—
cub

family of horses—
mare and colt

baby dog—
puppy

✔ To form the plural of most words that end in -f or -fe, change the -f or -fe to -v and add -es.

baby goose—
gosling

Baby Animals

(1) Baby cows are called _____.

(2) The young of _____ are cubs.

(3) Goslings are the _____ of geese.

(4) _____ of horses include colts.

(5) And dogs, of course, have _____.

Possessives—'s and s'

① Belongs to One

Use 's to show ownership by one person, place, thing, or group.

✔ Joe<u>'s</u> team was leading. (one Joe)

✔ The team<u>'s</u> coach cheered. (one team)

✔ Charles<u>'s</u> voice joined him. (one Charles)

Note: If the owner's name already ends in –s, it is also correct to just an an apostrophe. (Charles')

RULE OF THUMB!

Use 's to show ownership by a single person, place, thing, or group.

①

RULE OF THUMB!

Use s' to show ownership by more than one person, place, thing, or group.

②

② Belongs to More

Use s' to show ownership by two or more people, places, things, or groups.

✔ Both teams<u>'</u> records are good. (two teams)

✔ The students<u>'</u> spirit has helped. (many students)

Practice With a Purpose
Rule and Reference

Possessives— 's and s'

Possessives—'s and s'

Copy each sentence.

Choose the correct possessive.

(1) Theodor Geisel—do you recognize this (author's/authors') name?

(2) His (children's/childrens') books are among the (world's/worlds') best-known and loved.

(3) You may have heard of (Theodor's/Theodors') Lorax or Sneetches?

(4) Or, perhaps you have heard of his (Grinch's/Grinchs') grim deeds!

(5) Many (book's/books') pages were penned under this (master's/masters') preferred name—Dr. Seuss!

✓ Use 's to show ownership by a single person, place, thing, or group.

✓ Use s' to show ownership by more than one person, place, thing, or group.

Practice With a Purpose
Follow-up and Practice

Possessives—
'**s and s**'

Help With *ie* and *ei*

① Who's on First?

Generally, use *i* before *e*, except after *c*, or when it sounds like *a* as in *weigh*.

✔ Have a piece of cake.   (*i* before *e*)
✔ I believe it is chocolate.   (*i* before *e*)

✔ My neighbor brought it over. (*ei* sounds like *a*)
✔ She received a cookbook for her birthday. (*ei* after *c*)
✔ A friend gave it to her. (*i* before *e*)

Use *i* before *e* — except after *c*, or when the vowel pair sounds like *a*, or is "weird." OK?

①

② WEIRD Exceptions

The following words do not follow the rules.   The best thing to do is simply learn these WEIRD exceptions.

weird   either   neither   seize   leisure   their

Practice With a Purpose
Rule and Reference

Help With
ie* and *ei

Help With *ie* and *ei*

Rewrite the story so that it is spelled correctly.

Use *i* before *e* — except after *c*, or when the vowel pair sounds like *a*, or is "weird." OK?

Uninvited Guest

(1)My freind and I were having lunch on the porch and had gone inside briefly to refill our drinks. (2)When we returned, a piece of my sandwich was missing. (3)Suddenly we heard a weird rustling sound in a nearby bush. (4)Believing it to be the nieghbor's cat, we peeked into the bush. (5)Imagine when we found, to our surprise, that the thief was not a cat, but an opossum who had decided to drop by for lunch.

Practice With a Purpose
Follow-up and Practice

Help With
ie and *ei*

Not the Same—*Then/Than; Of /Have*

① **When? Then!**

Then means *when.* *Than* is used to compare. Never use *than* when you mean *then.* (Memory trick: then = when)

✔ My hair is longer *than* yours. (compares)
✔ I got sick and *then* went home. (when)
✗ It's farther *then* that. (compares—*than*)

Then means when. *Than compares.*

② **You Never Could Of**

Never use *of* when you mean *have.* You might *have,* but you never might *of,* must *of,* could *of,* would *of,* or should *of!*

✔ I should *have* seen it coming.
✗ I should *of* seen it coming.

RULE OF THUMB!

Do not use *of* when you mean *have.*

Practice With a Purpose
Rule and Reference

Not the Same—
Then / Than; Of / Have

Not the Same—*Then / Than; Of /Have*

Read carefully. Copy the poem, correcting each substitution of *then* for *than* and *of* for *have*.

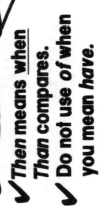

(1) I could of been an actress.
     I might of been a star!

(2) I could have been in movies.
     I could of gone so far!

(3) I could have been more famous
     Then anyone today.

(4) I could have signed more autographs
     Then anyone can say!

(5) But even though I *could* have,
     I went another way.

✔ *Then* means when
     Than compares.
✔ Do not use *of* when
     you mean *have*.

---

92   FS-10171 Plain English—Spelling

Prickly Pairs

① What's the Difference?

Some words present problems because th sound similar, yet have different meanings and spellings. Watch out for these!

RULE OF THUMB!

Check the spelling against the intended meaning.

✔

capital—a city
capitol—a building

accept—receive
except—leave out

loose—not tight
lose—misplace, not win

medal—an award
metal—a mineral

desert—a dry region
dessert—treat after a meal

already—previously
all ready—all are ready

past—already happened
passed—moved ahead of

stationary—in a fixed position
stationery—writing paper

Practice With a Purpose
Rule and Reference

Prickly Pairs

FS-10171 Plain English—Spelling

Prickly Pairs

Write each riddle correctly spelled. Then solve the riddle.

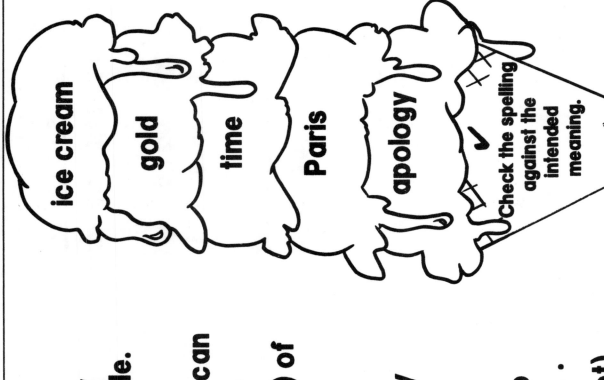

ice cream

gold

time

Paris

apology

Check the spelling against the intended meaning.

1. If you (lose/loose) me, I can never be returned. I am ___.

2. I am the (capital/capitol) of France. I am ___.

3. I am a popular (desert/dessert) that comes in many flavors. I am ___.

4. I am a precious (medal/metal) that caused a rush to California in 1849. I am ___.

5. You often (accept/except) me from someone who is sorry. I am an ___.

Practice With a Purpose
Follow-up and Practice

Prickly Pairs

Individual Record Sheet—Spelling

Name _____ Date begun _____ Student # _____

1. Sound-Alikes *Its* and *It's*

# correct		20%	40%	60%	80%	100%		
Pre-test	0	1	2	3	4	5		
Practice	0 1	2 3	4 5	6 7	8	9 10		
Post-test	0	1	2	3	4	5		

2. Sound-Alikes *Your* and *You're*

# correct		20%	40%	60%	80%	100%		
Pre-test	0	1	2	3	4	5		
Practice	0 1	2 3	4 5	6 7	8	9 10		
Post-test	0	1	2	3	4	5		

3. Sound-Alikes *Whose* and *Who's*

# correct		20%	40%	60%	80%	100%		
Pre-test	0	1	2	3	4	5		
Practice	0 1	2 3	4 5	6 7	8	9 10		
Post-test	0	1	2	3	4	5		

4. Sound-Alikes *There, Their,* and *They're*

# correct		20%	40%	60%	80%	100%		
Pre-test	0	1	2	3	4	5		
Practice	0 1	2 3	4 5	6 7	8	9 10		
Post-test	0	1	2	3	4	5		

5. Sound-Alikes *To, Two,* and *Too*

# correct		20%	40%	60%	80%	100%		
Pre-test	0	1	2	3	4	5		
Practice	0 1	2 3	4 5	6 7	8	9 10		
Post-test	0	1	2	3	4	5		

6. Plurals–Adding *-es*

# correct		20%	40%	60%	80%	100%		
Pre-test	0	1	2	3	4	5		
Practice	0 1	2 3	4 5	6 7	8	9 10		
Post-test	0	1	2	3	4	5		

7. Plurals–Making Changes

# correct		20%	40%	60%	80%	100%		
Pre-test	0	1	2	3	4	5		
Practice	0 1	2 3	4 5	6 7	8	9 10		
Post-test	0	1	2	3	4	5		

8. Possessives–Adding *-'s* and *-s'*

# correct		20%	40%	60%	80%	100%		
Pre-test	0	1	2	3	4	5		
Practice	0 1	2 3	4 5	6 7	8	9 10		
Post-test	0	1	2	3	4	5		

9. Help With *ie* and *ei*

# correct		20%	40%	60%	80%	100%		
Pre-test	0	1	2	3	4	5		
Practice	0 1	2 3	4 5	6 7	8	9 10		
Post-test	0	1	2	3	4	5		

10. Not the Same–*Then / Than; Of / Have*

# correct		20%	40%	60%	80%	100%		
Pre-test	0	1	2	3	4	5		
Practice	0 1	2 3	4 5	6 7	8	9 10		
Post-test	0	1	2	3	4	5		

11. Prickly Pairs (Common Mix-ups)

# correct		20%	40%	60%	80%	100%		
Pre-test	0	1	2	3	4	5		
Practice	0 1	2 3	4 5	6 7	8	9 10		
Post-test	0	1	2	3	4	5		

UNIT TEST—Spelling

# correct		20%	40%	60%	80%	100%		
Test	0 1	2 3	4 5	6 7	8	9 10		

Name _____ **Date** _____ **Score** _____

Spelling Checkup

Read the story. Underline 10 errors in spelling. Rewrite the story correctly on the lines below. Circle the changes you made.

Sand Dunes

Have you seen sand dunes in desserts or on beachs and wondered how they could of formed? What could move the wieght of all that heavy sand?

Actually these mounds are formed by the winds powerful forces pushing around trillions of sand grains. They're shapes are determined by wind direction.

But no dune shape lasts to long—it's shape is constantly changing as the wind shifts. So, If your going to admire a dune who's shape you especially like, you had better take a picture!

_____

_____

_____

_____

_____

_____

_____

_____

_____

_____

_____

_____

_____

_____

_____

_____

ANSWERS—FOLD UNDER BEFORE DUPLICATING: 1. desserts–deserts; 2. beachs–beaches; 3. (could) of–(could) have; 4. wieght–weight; 5. winds–wind's; 6. They're–Their; 7. to–too; 8. it's–its; 9. your–you're; 10. who's–whose